New Caribbean Poetry

KEI MILLER was born in Jamaica in 1978. He is the author of a collection of poetry, *Kingdom of Empty Bellies* (Heaventree Press, 2006), and a short fiction collection, *The Fear of Stones and Other Stories* (Macmillan, 2006). He has been a visiting writer at York University in Canada and a Vera Ruben Fellow at the Yaddo artists' community in the United States.

To f-

New Caribbean Poetry

An Anthology

edited by
KEI MILLER

CARCANET

First published in Great Britain in 2007 by
Carcanet Press Limited
Alliance House
Cross Street
Manchester M2 7AQ

A CIP catalogue record for this book is available from the British Library
ISBN 978 1 85754 941 6

The publisher acknowledges financial assistance from Arts Council England

Typeset by XL Publishing Services, Tiverton
Printed and bound in England by SRP Ltd, Exeter

Contents

Introduction

Recently I had to fight my way through JFK International airport. I finally emerged on the outside to a friend who had been patiently waiting. He greeted me with, 'What's good?' It seemed strange to me, this greeting. It could only accommodate a positive response. There was no space in it to say I was tired, harassed, hungry. In 'What's good?' was a demand for optimism.

Having arrived in New York to finish the present anthology, I decided there was indeed reason for optimism. What's good in Caribbean poetry today? I have eight answers: Tanya Shirley, Christian Campbell, Ian Strachan, Loretta Collins Klobah, Marilène Phipps-Kettlewell, Jennifer Rahim, Shara McCallum and Delores Gauntlett.

At first I thought I was putting together an anthology of 'emerging' poets, but that would have been an insult to those gathered here. At the time of writing, McCallum, Gauntlett and Rahim are completing their third books. Phipps-Kettlewell is onto her second. Collins Klobah and Campbell have manuscripts which have already won for both of them high placings and honourable mentions in prestigious competitions. Strachan has written one very good novel – my first introduction to his voice – and Tanya Shirley, who did her MFA at the University of Maryland, has been a fellow both at the Callaloo Writers' Workshop and at University of Pittsburgh's prestigious Cave Canem Summer Retreat. The poets here are not so much 'emerging' as 'newly emerged'. Indeed, they are New Caribbean Poets and theirs is New Caribbean Poetry. I chose this slightly more expansive and inclusive term 'Caribbean' instead of 'West Indian'. Traditionally, the latter has been used as a designation only of the English-speaking countries in the region. In this small selection however, both the Francophone and the Hispanophone Caribbean are represented; Marilène Phipps-Kettlewell is Haitian and Loretta Collins Klobah writes out of Puerto Rico. Still, they are writing in English, and so if I speak of a regional canon, I'm speaking generally of a Caribbean canon, but specifically a West Indian one.

It is generally accepted that excellent West Indian Literature only began to appear in the 1900s. In the three or four hundred years before that, Caribbean territories were occupied – by European colonists who didn't see themselves as belonging to the Caribbean; by African slaves who were also longing for another home and, in any case, were not allowed to read or write; and by indentured labourers from China and India who arrived relatively late in the game. The world met itself in the Caribbean (as George Lamming might tell us), but it would take a while for the various peoples not to see themselves as belonging 'elsewhere'. People, customs, languages had to come together and cross-pollinate; new dialects had to be spoken; new rituals created;

various national cultures, subcultures and, importantly, tensions had to be formed and, finally, out of that, a national literature. It took a while for that literature to begin, and then a longer while for it to become good.

Derek Walcott from St Lucia, and Kamau Brathwaite from Barbados are seen as the two foremost West Indian poets. Walcott was awarded the Nobel Prize in 1992. His work is known for a rootedness in an English/European tradition which he has rightly embraced as an equal part of his heritage. Brathwaite, on the other hand, seems more committed to forging 'something new'. He famously states 'the hurricane does not roar in pentameter', suggesting that an old form would never fit nor adequately represent a new world. He argues for a new rhythm and meter and style. But Walcott as the Western traditionalist, and Brathwaite as the innovative Africanist, are distinctions that are more popular than they are true; any additional reading will complicate these supposed differences, at the same time highlighting many similarities between the two. Still, whether fairly or not, they have come to represent two separate camps in West Indian poetry, and at one point all poets emerging from the region, it seemed, had to choose an allegiance. One of the markers of the eight new Caribbean poets featured here is a refusal to make any such choice, a willingness to be influenced, even significantly, by both, and indeed by a whole host of other poets not necessarily from the Caribbean. Such an expansiveness of influence can only be positive as will be certainly evident in the quality of poetry found here.

Walcott and Brathwaite started publishing in the 1950s and 60s respectively. During that time, and in the twenty years that followed, many other major Caribbean poets emerged: Martin Carter, Grace Nichols, John Agard and Fred D'Aguiar from Guyana, Kendel Hipollyte from St Lucia, Dennis Scott, Mervyn Morris, Lorna Goodison, Olive Senior and Linton Kwesi Johnson from Jamaica, Wayne Brown and Dionne Brand from Trinidad, Merle Collins from Grenada. These names have been inducted into a West Indian literary canon, and as is the case with all canons, scholarship has gone back to them again and again. Unintentionally perhaps, this becomes a kind of gate-keeping – a way to keep those in, safely in. Every once in a while, however, we must look in another, less safe direction. We must look to the noise we have been ignoring – for at the gate other poets are brandishing large stones, banging, trying to get our attention. The more subversive ones are trying to remove the gate altogether. We must look to these poets who lay legitimate claim to a tradition which they are, at the same time, expanding and reinventing. The present anthology introduces eight such who in the past ten years or less have been doing this.

On the back cover of Shara McCallum's first book, *The Water Between Us*, there is a disagreement which may begin to support my assertion that influences have become more expansive, and as such, lineages have become wonderfully messy. Kwame Dawes says McCallum's work is the 'closest thing to a marriage between [the African-American] Lucille Clifton and [the Jamaican poet] Lorna Goodison'. Michael Waters, on the other hand, agrees about Clifton but says the other half of the union is Derek Walcott. Of course neither critic is trying to imply that the poet's voice is the product of only two 'parents' and not indeed the product of every voice (poetic or otherwise) they have internalised. For my part, I don't see the clear stamp of Walcott on McCallum – not that I doubt his influence is there, and perhaps, how could it not be? But if, as I suspect, Waters meant to say McCallum's voice is distinctly Caribbean and distinctly good, then there is no disagreement. She claims a Caribbean identity despite not 'looking' Caribbean – at least, not in the exotifying gaze of a world that has made 'natives' only of the black and Indian populations. McCallum writes of an encounter with Bob Marley:

> ... Bob, who was only a brother in Twelve Tribes to me at four or five, said to the man who called me *whitey gal* that I was not, that I was a daughter of Israel, that I was Stair's child.
>
> ('What I'm Telling You', p. 88)

Jamaica is her home and she mourns having had to leave the island. In her 'mermaid sequence', you will find a powerful metaphor for migration and all its sadness: 'The tragedy of the mermaid'

> is not that she must leave her home
> but that she must cast off her flesh.
> To love, she must lose scales as a child
> relinquishes dolls to youth;
>
> ('The tragedy of the mermaid', p. 91)

and from another poem in the same cycle:

> With age, your hair will grow matted and dull,
> your skin will gape and hang in long folds,
> your eyes will cease to shine.
> But nothing will be enough.
> The sea will never take you back.
>
> ('What the Oracle Said', p.92)

Migration happens in the opposite direction for Loretta Collins Klobah and she disrupts simple notions of what is Caribbean and what is Caribbean poetry. Born in the United States, with an MFA from the prestigious Iowa Workshop, she has since claimed the Caribbean in much the way that

Caribbean people have claimed the rest of the world – Christian Campbell's 'Rudical':

> *Mine New Cross mine Oldham Notting Hill Bradford Brixton mine too*
> *Nassau Laventille Bridgetown Kingston*
>
> (p. 56)

Indeed, for Loretta Collins Klobah, hers is America, Puerto Rico, Jamaica, English, Spanish, Spanglish, Patois. She claims space and language without earnestness or apology, ironically, even when the poem is running away from the Caribbean:

> Yes, this poem is on the run –
> until the Caribbean is ready to greet this poem
>   like we meet friends in Puerto Rico, *with a besito –*
> *with a saludos, with an embrace.*
>   See what I mean?
>
> ('Going Up, Going Down', p. 61)

When she is the social critic, Collins Klobah never speaks from a place that is outside or superior. Her voice embodies the communal we, our, us:

> We have created a new world where the indiscriminate gun
> is always at our backs. From the first murdered *Taino* to now,
> the cosmic bullet has been in the air. The carved moon
> trots across the sky. Let us rock our babies
> to sleep, kissing their hair, rearranging
> their night clothes, playing our odds against
> carnage, against the stray shot seeking our thresholds.
>
> ('El Valerio, The Wake (1893), p. 59)

Like Lorna Goodison and Derek Walcott, Marilène Phipps-Kettlewell is a poet as well as a painter. Unlike her 'forebears' however, Phipps-Kettlewell is equally accomplished in both arts. If her work is 'Caribbean' it is because it is rooted in the actual land rather than in a regional canon. In a recent interview she was asked about the influence of other Haitian writers on her work and responded that there wasn't much: '[T]he people of Haiti themselves have influenced my work... the Kreyol language is expressed in, and sustained by, an incredible sense of imagery.' For Phipps-Kettlewell, the past and childhood are constant sources of inspiration:

> – 'When will my poem end? How can it end
> while fruits from my childhood still hang on trees

like ornaments of an inexhaustible Christmas?'

('Dialogue', p. 14)

What Phipps-Kettlewell does, however, share with Goodison is a refusal to shy away from the spiritual. Her poetry is in constant conversation with God, but this conversation is carried out in a language so fresh it never becomes mere rhetoric or even 'religious'. Phipps-Kettlewell's embrace of God is essentially an awareness of human frailty and smallness, and this awareness invites us to transcend ourselves:

Yet we too must go one day beyond ourselves
and realize at last what in fantasies and rites we had already

('On Good Friday', p. 19)

or she asks her readers to imagine themselves as a frog,

able to leap
a distance many times your own measure

('Frog', p. 4)

It is impossible not to see Brathwaite in the work of Ian Strachan. In his use of rhythm and physical layout (often intimately related to Brathwaite's) there is the echo of that great Barbadian's trilogy *The Arrivants*. Consider Brathwaite's 'Folkways' and Strachan's 'Mae Hanna, Grandmother' side by side:

I am a fuck-	'teacher
in' negro	wan'
man, hole	teach her
in my head,	more dan
brains in	da gold
my belly;	an'
black skin	rule'
red eyes	
broad back	bloodnight
big you know	man gone
what: not very quick	mangrove
	man grovin'
to take offence	stronger
but once	erry day
offended, watch	
that housee	whip
you livin' in	spawn

```
an' watch that lit-              ship
tle sister                       ho'n
              (Braithwaite)      of meager
                                 pay
                                        (Strachan)
```

Strachan weaves dialect, folksongs and even, if I may co-opt the suggestive term, 'drumspeak' into his work, but he does it effortlessly (or so the final product seems):

kadak doong doong
kakkadak doong doong

this is how the eyes begin
their easy retreat into the skull
how the muscles tighten and then relax
how the joints prepare themselves
for their starry passengers

kadak doong doong dak dak doong doong
        ('gods and spirits are summoned through the portal divine', p. 119)

Christian Campbell, another Bahamian, is a prodigious talent. He, more than any of the others, is trying out a variety of voices which range from the folk-centred talk about 'grandmummy', to a more world-wise and cynical description of Oxford, to the chant of a rent-a-dread (or is it Ras-titute?) prowling on a Caribbean beach. Even in fixed form his voice is still looking for new shapes. His sonnet, perhaps appropriately, resists the iambic (though not the pentameter) in favour of a rhythm closer to the two speakers' voices:

but he's Haitian and knows about fleeing.
I will get there fast. Learning that only
sea bounds us, our islands, he churns loose the sing
song of a kweyol-coated tongue. *Do you see*

yourself here for good?, I ask him. All I
catch is: *No. Port-au-Prince. Night. Stars. You know,
la lune.* How the stars dive for the dead, then rise.
How la lune bellies full as Toussaint's hope.
                                        ('Repatriation', p. 51)

Campbell is certainly conscious of himself and indeed the Caribbean subject being able to draw from and 'put on' various voices as different situations demand:

At immigration I put on airs
and styles...
                    I look
only ahead and walk straight-back,
like my grandfather. Speak like he spoke
to foreigners. In his best moods,
he would put on the mouths
of all the Englishmen he'd met,
playing the Queen and how
she gave him his MBE – Pa.

('Legba', p. 45)

Delores Gauntlett's work echoes much that I've liked in the American
formalist, Robert Hayden. In her poems that feature the figure of a father
wrecked by a war, scarred into silence, I often hear, playing in the back-
ground, Hayden's famous 'Those Winter Sundays'. That poem opens in the
reverie of observing a father wake to the ritual of work:

Sundays too my father got up early
and put his clothes on in the blueblack cold,
then with cracked hands that ached
from labor in the weekday weather made
banked fires blaze.

Gauntlett's 'A Song for My Father' (p. 24) begins in a similar conceit:

Against the yam-vine quiet of the garden
a nightingale stirred with my father: the lift
and fall of the pickaxe, the heaving throat
of the hidden bird exacting
the subtleties of song.
This would become the memory of high grass.

Near the end of Hayden's poem he cries, 'What did I know? What did I
know!' It is a lament that appears in Gauntlett's own work: 'Though what
did I know at eight/ about the bends they crossed' ('Pocomania', p. 34) What
Gauntlett shares with Hayden is not only a preference for pentametric lines,
but the powerful craft of nostalgia. Gauntlett does not long for the past (as
Dionne Brand would put it), steering far away from sentimentality. But what
she invokes and evokes so effectively, is a year that has already gone:

Now, under these scorched foundation stones,
lies the unstirred clay steeped in grandfather's life:

a life I never knew.
No photograph from which to root his face –
yet his nearness throbs
in the richness of a September noon.

('Under These Stones', p. 25)

I imagine if you asked Tanya Shirley what is it that makes a poem a poem, or a poet a poet, she might quote herself: 'It is the way you hold your mouth.' In this anthology she stands out as the most 'narrative'. This sensibility should not be dismissed, as some critics might, as a prose sensibility. Indeed, you must observe the way the poet holds her mouth, specifically, the way she holds her lines. Her poem 'Guinep' (p. 99), is a daring demonstration of the tension that can be achieved in lineation. The poem is not stanzaic; each line is set apart to earn its own place:

To eat a guinep you must first crack the skin

I am always aware of my mouth and how easily things slip in

There is a myth that follows the fruit like an after-bite

The child who swallows the seed must be turned upside down

The biographies of Shirley and McCallum are mirrored to a point. Both are Jamaican women. They both studied with Merle Collins at the University of Maryland. They both have been Cave Canem Fellows. To complete the circle, Shirley's current PhD work is partially concerned with McCallum's poetry. But whereas McCallum's most eloquent engagement with the theme of migration is in metaphor, Shirley finds her own eloquence in being more direct:

Just for remembrance, I talk patwa to the furniture.
…
Here, you must turn food into language.
Cook tin ackee and fresh codfish
until the aroma says,
'Mawning, how you do? Long time no see.'

('Sunday Ritual', p. 102)

Finally, there is Jennifer Rahim, who is somewhat responsible for this anthology. At a dinner one evening in Manchester, Michael Schmidt of Carcanet asked who were the exciting new poets in the Caribbean. Without hesitation, I answered: Jennifer Rahim. If the job of poetry is, as Shakespeare says, to give to airy nothings a local habitation and a name, then Rahim is a poet. She takes that very dictum and localises it to the Caribbean in her own recurring trope of the 'unbaptised douen' – the dead ghost of a child who must be given a name, a location, a home, in order to rest:

> he blessed their high intelligence
> to brave the abandoned places
> only to save what is theirs alone to give,
> blessed again and again that perfect beauty
> until the child became sunlight,
> forever shining within –
>
> ('Saint Francis and the Douen', p. 151)

Or if the job of poetry is, as Shelley says, to make the familiar, unfamiliar, but to make the unspectacular, spectacular, then again, Rahim is a poet. Read as a guide to Shelley's dictum, Rahim's 'Song':

> to the iron-board's unconsidered flatness, praise
> the necessity of clean, well-pressed cotton
> linen, denim, rayon – all fabrics, praise
> the vexed countenance of a wrinkled white blouse,
>
> ('Song', p. 138)

At a recent 'Gathering of Writers' held at the Mona campus of the University of the West Indies, Derek Walcott declared that Caribbean poetry was only just beginning. The greatness was yet to come. The eight poets featured here are perhaps a small representation of 'New Caribbean Poetry', but they are among the best. Their work is often featured in regional journals; they have been winning prizes; indeed, theirs are the names that are often called when one asks the question, what's good and new in Caribbean poetry? For despite 'the waters between us', poets in the region are often apart no more than one or two degrees of separation. Along such small chains, word quickly stumbles back about who is writing exciting things. These eight are; they are the beginning of Walcott's prophecy.

But indeed, eight is a small number. Every anthology, it seems, has to defend its exclusions. Usually the anthologist invokes the law of subjectivity. I do the same; in the following pages are poets to whose work I have been drawn by my own aesthetics, which, like all aesthetics, is a personal, limited, biased thing. But also, the ambition of the current project is a modest one. This anthology does not try to account for the whole length and breadth of the contemporary Caribbean poetry scene, but simply to feature and give a generous sampling of a few of its better practitioners.

Still, some absences feel more present than others and deserve note. Staceyann Chin, who has made a large name for herself on the Slam poetry circuit in North America, is a voice I would have welcomed. Chin is the twenty-first century's answer to the dub and protest poetry of the 1960s and 70s which introduced to the world poets such as Mikey Smith, Jean Binta Breeze and Benjamin Zephaniah. The genre, however, had since then sputtered into a dull silence, failing to produce anything remarkable. With the middle class throughout the Caribbean suddenly more 'coloured-ful', and politicians no longer English, poems which continue to blame 'whitey' or 'England' seem derivative and disingenuous. Chin has, however, moved on. She has replaced the 'colonial' with the heterosexual – a move which has made her the typical prophetess shunned in her own (homophobic) hometown. One might dare to call it an 'advantage', as the position of standing outside a closed and unwelcoming door has lent her work urgency. If something is added to her poetry by a histrionic, though always engaging, performance, in the best of her work there is a hurt that takes shape.

While Delores Gauntlett is featured in these pages, so too could be many of the other participants from Wayne Brown's workshops. Brown is an irascible and stubborn man who is equally generous in sharing both his snobberies and his insights. In other words, he is the very best kind of poetry teacher there can be – always demanding from his students a newness and freshness that is still grounded. Judging from the accomplishments of poets who emerge from the cocoon of his tutorials, one might soon have to call Brown a father of contemporary Jamaican (if not Caribbean) poetry. Poets from his workshops include Frances Coke, Gwyneth Barber-Wood, Millicent Graham, Verna George and Raymond Mair. However, like the poets from another successful workshop in Jamaica – the Calabash group – for my purposes they suffered the single disadvantage of being Jamaican, a group I was careful not to over-represent.

The young Guyanese writer Ruel Johnson is also not here, but I would like to shine a brief spotlight on him: a couple of years ago, not much more than twenty years old, Johnson created a sensation by being shortlisted in two categories of the Guyana Prize for Literature. He submitted self-published manuscripts in the poetry and fiction categories and was successful in fiction, becoming the youngest winner of the Prize. I agree with the results; Johnson is more accomplished in prose than he is in poetry, and were this an anthology of New Caribbean Prose, his work would certainly have been featured.

Still there are others who have written or performed a poem that moved me: Lynne Procope, Roger Bonair-Agard, Lelewatte Manoo-Rahming. There must also be those I just haven't read or heard yet. According to Jennifer Rahim, there are rare bamboo patches scattered around these islands where we gather. But the Caribbean is a wide space and I do not know all of these patches, nor all the voices that haunt them. Open mike events abound in Jamaica, Trinidad, Puerto Rico, the Cayman Islands and Barbados. There have been several workshops: a philanthropic organisation in Trinidad, the Cropper Foundation, has so far sponsored four of these for emerging Caribbean writers. Before them, there was the Caribbean Writers' Summer Institute at the University of Miami. The Cave Hill Summer Arts Workshops are held regularly in Barbados. Ongoing creative writing courses are taught at the University of the West Indies and an MFA programme has recently been established on the St Augustine Campus. Journals such as *Anthurium*, *Calabash*, *Callaloo* and *Caribbean Writer* are yet other spaces where poets from the region are establishing themselves. Eight poets are featured here, but I hope they will encourage you to look for what else is new and good in Caribbean poetry.

When I arrived at JFK International, it was as the 2006 Vera Rubin Fellow at Yaddo. It was at this fellowship that I completed the present anthology. Going through the submissions, discovering and deciding on poems, putting them together, was both a pleasure and somewhat of a humbling experience. How, as a reader, could I not smile at Marilène Phipps-Kettlewell's 'Frog' or Tanya Shirley's 'My Christian Friend'? How, as a poet myself, could I come face to face with the work of Delores Gauntlett or Shara McCallum, and not feel wonderfully humbled?

It was also in New York that when old friends from back home kept asking, 'Kei, what's good?', I could respond with the optimism they demanded: 'Have you ever heard of Tanya Shirley? Jennifer Rahim? Christian Campbell? Ian Strachan? Marilène Phipps-Kettlewell? Loretta Collins Klobah? Delores Gauntlett? Shara McCallum?'

Here they are. Enjoy.

Kei Miller

MARILÈNE PHIPPS-KETTLEWELL

MARILÈNE PHIPPS-KETTLEWELL is a painter, a poet and a short story writer who was born and grew up in Haiti. She has held fellowships at the Guggenheim Foundation, and at the Bunting Institute, the W.E.B. Du Bois Institute for Afro-American Research and the Center for the Study of World Religions at Harvard, and has been the recipient of a grant from the New England Foundation for the Arts. In 1993 she won the Grolier Prize for poetry. Her poetry collection *Crossroads and Unholy Water* (Southern Illinois University Press, 2000) won the 1999 Crab Orchard poetry prize. (It was also a finalist for the Walt Whitman prize from the Academy of American Poets.) Marilène Phipps-Kettlewell has published six books of poetry, and her work has appeared in magazines such as *Callaloo*, *Ploughshares* and *River Styx* and in the anthologies *Sisters of Caliban: Contemporary Women Poets of the Caribbean* (Azul Editions, 1996) and *The Beacon Best of 1999* (Beacon Press). Her short fiction was selected for *The Best American Short Stories 2003*, as well as listed in *The Best American Short Stories 2001*.

Sanctuary

I name this a Sanctuary. Enter.
I want you to bare your feet –
you must feel the difference of ground.
Your eyes must accommodate the light –
let it be alien.
All breathing must accommodate the silence,
a quiet in the understanding of clouds,
your hands a fragrant, needful folly.
What descends here has heart within lead.
There is no blood here, but fluid courses.
There are no guardians here, but you are perceived.
There is no fire here, but my love.

Frog

If it could be done, would you want
to be made into a frog?
If it meant having a thin-boned spine,
gray-green humid skin that feels
the sting of any slight insect you might
otherwise gobble and swallow,
sit the world apart
in a wide, four-legged sweaty squat,
the beating of your heart showing in your throat,
and yet be able to leap
a distance many times your own measure.

If it meant you can enter water
more vast than your body can ever swim through and,
nevertheless relaxed, arms and legs stretched open,
like a molecule afloat,
round eyes absorbing the world
through greenish inner screens that draw
towards and within you
the soft slithering silk of the water's surface,
the slosh and sway of high palm leaves,
defiant birds gathered in the immense blue and,
even then, still be able to stare at the sun.

And if it also meant you could dive deep in the far depth of the water,
go down, down to where there is no bottom, none to feel or reach,
down to an infinity of movement that requires no breath.

If it could be done and it meant you would
know love, would you come,
to be born a Man? Or even, woman?

The Christ is Born

If I were to follow the only star on earth
because the sky has fallen over
and God no longer adds from above,
what would I offer Forgiveness newly-born?
What is in me to return that has fragrance?

Footprints circle in the snow
at the park – black islands dizzying
around a single tree – each man is an island.

Cloaked in black throughout life,
each monk enclosed in his island of prayer
espouses the beginning of self in God.
Does the year have a place of beginning
in one's heart for whom God is the only place?
Where do monks' footsteps lead?
Will they be laid in the grave wearing white?

Where there is no absolution, there is sorrow –
sin ill-forgiven digs the flesh –
forgiveness is self-effacing.
Pride climbs its death-driven steps all year long
to come at last to bend at the Crèche.

Monks enter the Chapel.
Their being impresses itself there
before sepulchral time puts its claim
for each to be dissolved
like footprints in the snow and
only a sheet of earth remains.
They walk in black files towards the seat of prayer
like migrating birds seen from afar.
Their chants – monotonous, passive,
repetitious calls – are in single praise
for the divine whiteness who spread snow
to recognize our steps.
Each step we take tells anew what we are:
an island, an imprint, a direction.

Chapel Space

In a space where beings are transparencies of color
born out of a stone-chiseled struggle for form,
hard and pale, with better substance to endure through time,
then elevated to a pillared position that establishes a difference
between us below – uncomfortably sitting, recognizable
through an illusory favor that reveals us
as wrapped, robed, stiffened, uncertain, shifting mounds
bound within thread-stitched layers of charismatic cloth –
in such a space, is there place for prayer that burns to rest
in a candid dance for the remembrance of those flimsy and slight
who carry in their changeable faces the body of my heart's life –
these memories woven through them,
born out of solitude and born of bliss?

Come Visit

Come visit this life and enter
to remark, dispel and enchant.
A lamp with a large shade illuminates all that lies under.
But go easy with your given body of a beast –
a heart pulses close under the skin,
wanting to be touched.
Notice: I have given you more, and other, than that which you desired;
still, don't refuse me – I am in all that comes
and every second of time unfolds like a hand.
Do not ask for this you choose – love awakening – to stop,
rather to linger, and remain close to your breast always.
Allow yourself to be a night marauder over what is boxed and tightly sealed,
keep your lantern lit as you descend in the graves –
there are such dreams left untapped in one, embalmed and entombed early.

On a Cross

Mother of God! Your child
has been hung at your feet, on a cross.
Cry a mother's tears for mothers who own a bloodied child.
Cry for every infant grown old to die alone without his mother's grief for
anchor.
Cry for those who lived without heart and died before your son ever lived.
Cry! Mother of God!
Because common children live from their mothers' tears,
and tears of common mothers are used up long before their children's use
of them.

Cry, but for me, do not cry,
for one has selflessly died for me:
his death will be the company of my death after being that of my life.
Mother, do not cry,
because such a death as your child's
was lived to tell all how to live,
and gives each one a new heart.

Hear

Dear God, take this entire body – I no longer need it,
I have not used it well, it was not mine to own alone.
Better that I am altogether gone
than to find you missing in my house.
Better I cease to exist than to remain in your absence.

Rivers that cross men's towns seek an estuary.
So, when evening lassitude brings in torpor through the senses,
vacillation to the heart, and erasures in the mind, is it sleep?
Or is it a friend who penetrates and frees the entire being
from old stooges used to lord there?

If so, come! Disarticulate me whole!
I want to feel your loving form,
be pulled open and fall into a night that blackens all,
and throws me, vanquished, into your luminous desire.
Once there, I want to hear your Word, I want to know
        who you are.

May You Live

May you live long, long,
to a blossomed, handsome patriarchal age,
the blue light of sea in your eyes
inundating fields you traverse.

May your love irretrievably spent
gather around you in forms you can touch,
heaven knowing fully
that both well and spring
in each created being are fed from the same water,
there meant to collect so it can overflow.

This earth welcomes your weight
and resonates with each step your heart takes,
knowing itself to be a woman able,
and only brought to life,
when your breath feels her face
like a blind man reading.

The Ink of My Heart

The ink of my heart shows red and pours over the entire page –

This heart enshrines Love with words,
then pulls away like the tide
to reveal red roses, genuflected on the sand where seagulls cry.

Each man is but a bottle at sea, a letter enclosed.

Each man is an ocean that generates these encapsulated cries
like burgeons of a mind,
fallen and abandoned over waves.

For each telling attempted, the ocean awakens.
It opens a heart encumbered by reefs through which other lives circulate.
Hurt halts for an infinite moment when a hesitant hand holds the parchment
with timeless regard for its anemone's tenderness and texture.

Blue Eyes

There is one eye at the bottom of the ocean.
Man in his boat leans over to see its color
and gets inscribed. Memory is something written.
God saw what he had done and it was good.
Since then, to belong means to be accountable:
don't reject, don't wound, don't betray
the one who saw you, and paused.
The ocean's eye recognizes you:
in every single scale of the fish
that knows you are in the boat above,
your remembered face glistens.

The other eye is in the sky –
you have to raise yourself to see it.
Distant birds' black wings
trace the alphabet of emotions
in God. When that eye cries,
fine fruits swell on trees.
It is in the eyes that
love rests and remains.

Estuary

Our friends go like leaves of a season.
They slide out of the screen with all their colors
and the theater is brought back to ordinary life.
Bumblebees go heavily from one flower to the next;
they steal what is considered there most fine.

Absence hollows a heart
that finds in itself an excess of empty space,
so it drags everything towards its breast like a wide-arm estuary
grateful for all manner of ships that whistle in
and grace its shores with the novel whiteness of sails.

The heart gives in to this busy lull
until wind and tide ally themselves
to drain it out anew,
draw its shores with larger, wider strokes,
and reveal a previously unimagined, unseen depth.

Dialogue

– 'Return to your home: in your childhood, in your heart.
Beyond the present of your being, that is where you live.
The desire for sleep overwhelms you: it is fear.'
– 'But what peace can there be in this dizzy of sensations?'
– 'Sing, and you will recognize your voice:
in the charmed, puffed-up tutus of ballet dancers,
many sounds await their time in you
since the beginning of your sun.'
– 'When will my poem end? How can it end
while fruits from my childhood still hang on trees
like ornaments of an inexhaustible Christmas?'
– 'Understand that a lustrous, fat cat's paw
will deliciously strike them down in one distracted, dry pat.'
– 'So, just like mice, we are its daily fare? And yet,
before I must leave, I want my friends' voices to return to the foliage,
see their large faces hang like talismans on my wide open arms,
hear their love tell that, for them, I have lived.'

Birds

Sky and dreams share the same limitless screen.
Brave birds live there, they fashion themselves in our image.
Their laughter carries over vast distances.
Like thoughts about the coming fall, they suddenly
migrate in hordes from the invisible heavens,
flying in uneven strips of dotted black lace.

Luminous clouds gather above, unreachable,
but all can be held in a single drop of rain,
as it falls into the palm of our hand.
Our mind seeks sleep, while we only need
our heart to see
the immaterial face we love.

Is it ever understood
that a family on earth is only birds, partners in play,
shrill and driven by the chance of streams,
held by the strength of their wings?

Is it ever understood
that each one of us is but a bird
choosing, or not, to rest in the dream-thought
of another's heart,
halted in its flight for a moment down below?

Lobsters

Humanity living with its lobster heads
ripped daily in back-alleys' kabuki,
each meager dragon face, an odorous discarded mask,
eyes dangling free, like night ornaments
blackened, bleak and blind.

As it is disarmed of its gripping claws,
the creature is then bereft of its armor –
a crisp, brittle shell with a glass-like delicacy –
that reveals its naked center as flesh,
coiled pink like a heart prepped for Valentine.

The once fiercely flapping tail, now an empty husk,
shows a transparency the color of a tropical dusk.
Thus it is cast-off with its never-revealed dreams
of thrilling birds in flight across a peach dawn horizon,
embroidered with the black winter thread of distant branching trees.

The Life of Small Ones

I Starfish

Like a gem fallen from the night sky,
then ejected from the ocean,
hard-spined, yet obsolete,
the starfish weighs lightly on the sand.
Gulls flip it in glee
and stare inside its limbs:
exposed, provoked and pained by the new glare,
the starfish lets out an insistent scent of sea,
the way madmen tenaciously repeat a single word
that names the hollow they feel inside.

II Dark Ants

Watch for thieves prostrate in idolatrous covenants,
disjointed in their appeals for the recovery of vice,
like dark ants that indiscriminately sting
to delineate their zones of control.
They scurry about with bounty bigger than themselves
that they must at last deliver to a live treasure chest –
a queen that daily swells from greed and glee

III Fireflies

An evanescent summer dance of fireflies
is a charm exquisite and light. Well-intended
with built-in bulbs,
they finger the air in zigzags
without an apparent plan.
But when the hour has come
and their senses are informed by darkness,
funny that it should be from their poor-in-spirit
rear-ends, that a designed illumination bursts forth.

A Chicken

A chicken has settled atop my father's tomb.

Standing stiff on yellow feet, it began
the survey of this bare-earth rectangle
as if it was a vast domain, its very own.

It then took a pause to appraise
how straight the great tree is
at the foot of which the grave was dug.

Head held in profile
like a question mark with a yellow eye,
it looked up at the trunk to its full height
all the way to an expanse of foliage
that softly filtered light
dappling the ground below.

Watching it in its chicken dance
scratching the earth one foot after the other,
I thought it wanted a worm.

But no – satisfied with just the hole it dug,
full of presumption and certainty,
over it the chicken sat.

Its tail made like a fan behind its thin head
and also seemed as an arrow that pointed upwards
to the wooden cross overhanging.

Only the carved name and dates can be read:
1919–1996
The chicken will not lay seventy-seven eggs.
Not even seven. Would it lay only three,
or just one, that would be plenty.

On Good Friday

The long black line of livestock in a procession towards the slaughterhouse
resembles that made by monks who walk to the altar in silence,
two by two
like Noah's chosen:
they kneel down three times on the way,
and prostrate themselves each time.

At last, they espouse the earth at the foot of the cross
which they kiss with thin, offered lips,
thus making out of death,
in which they see themselves, find and join each other,
the Arch that lifts them, saves them
out of the terrestrial malediction,
and leads them to a place more propitious to true life.

Wild rabbits or mice, we are hardly better – easily frightened,
fleeing from all that presents itself as greater than us,
as shadow, as image, as gesture.
Yet we too must go one day beyond ourselves,
and realize at last what in fantasies and rites we had already
accomplished – live the death that demands the gift
of a live heart that knows how to expand
within a body that knew only how to shrink.

DELORES GAUNTLETT

DELORES GAUNTLETT was born and grew up in Jamaica, where she still lives. Her poetry has appeared in magazines and anthologies including *The Caribbean Writer*, *Poetry News* (London), *Kunapipi*, *The Jamaica Observer*, *Jamaica Journal*, *Hampden-Sydney Poetry Review*, *Bayswater-Germany*, *Calabash* and *The Sunday Gleaner*. She has published two books of poetry, *Freeing Her Hands To Clap* (*The Jamaica Observer*, 2001), winner of the 2000 National Book Development Council/Una Marson Biannual Award, and *The Watertank Revisited* (Peepal Tree, 2005). She was awarded the 1999 David Hough prize and has been a multiple winner in the *Jamaica Observer* annual poetry competition. In 2006 Delores Gauntlett received the 2006 Daily News prize from *The Caribbean Writer*.

The Carpenter

To see him as he was is easy.
Knowing he can no longer do the things
he once did is harder to realize –
and the day his legs buckled under him
is naked in my mind. That day,
he arrived to do his last job outside the house
with more than average confidence,
perhaps a cover for the drawl in his approach.
How he sprung up at once into
the same *good morning* smile, though
I know now he was not himself,
that it was the revelation of how swiftly
the cancer was spreading
that spilled from his eyes.
(That look said a thousand things,
and seemed to say them all to me
as though I'd eavesdropped on his mind.)
I watched him brush away the awkwardness
which swept the sawdust floor.
He refused my offer of a sweet drink,
a glass of lemonade I thought would quell
the wake of the look that said, *I want to pass
alone through this* – to face the door
from which the light of another morning
will frame things as they are, or were.

A Song for My Father

Against the yam-vine quiet of the garden
a nightingale stirred with my father: the lift
and fall of the pickaxe, the heaving throat
of the hidden bird exacting
the subtleties of song.
This would become the memory of high grass
brushing wet against black waterboots.

I didn't realize I was watching him
when, as to an altar
he bent with bare hands to a sudden digging
till the head of yam surfaced
like a flowering from the earth;
the nightingale's song perched
upon the senses, then drifted
from the dewy pimento leaves
and, like a scent, was gone.

Under These Stones

This is the spot where the walls stood:
my father's father's house
destroyed by fire
where the smell of beet-red coffee berries filled the air
and the smoke went up in silence.

The house I visited, the year
my father could not bring his father back,
is now either a memory or this brambled pit,
the footpath to it overrun by leaf-of-life
whose stems we'd strip to make stick dolls.

Now, under these scorched foundation stones,
lies the unstirred clay steeped in grandfather's life:
a life I never knew.
No photograph from which to root his face –
yet his nearness throbs
in the richness of a September noon.

Every memory must break somewhere –
the air palpable with the grace of a drinking hen
strutting to its nest with a promise to fulfill,
the clucking in the shadow of banana leaves
that glistened with morning dew –
no telling what time was or where it went –
the days replete with trees to climb.

Interview with a Centenarian

They pressed him for his secret
to having lived so long,
looking past him and all he'd said thus far:
When he looks out the window
there's no one watering the flower bed,
that still, he writes her name in window-mist.
And gradually taken, one by one,
his children and his friends
so in night's silence he sits
on the edge of the bed
with her smile
tucked in his shirt.

You're a lucky man, they told him.
His eyes said not.
And still they pressed for an answer
pushing past his words
as past a drift of fallen leaves
stepping across
as though it were something to be stumbled on
in a single sentence.

They did not read his eyes or hear him say
that packing a lifetime in fifteen minutes
would be like holding water in his hand,
that he spoke of silences
from which his memory feeds. Still
they pressed.
Not wanting to call anything by name
he said I live because I have not died.

Doctorbird

A resonance of woodland green
and black, he swept past
at shimmering speed to pause
                midair
in the winged parenthesis of what keeps him hovering:
his red beak dipped in curiosity
probing the throat of the ripe banana shoot
in the corner of my father's garden.

A rush of grace, of the hummingbird-kind,
climbing up and down upon an empty space
too busy to perch, to be pinned to one spot,
he is the only bird to fly sideways
and back
like thought
yet I've never heard him sing;

just the cautious humming from his wings
brushing against the breeze.
Scarcely bigger than a thumb
the leaves stirred in his wake like a fluttering heart,
a proof within how little it takes
to lend adjustment to the door
of what makes a child resume playing.

The Empty House

The flash of familiar things
unwinds the past like a ball of string
enough to bridge the gap between my father's death
and my accepting no one would ever know
his final thoughts, alone in that red settee
between the time my mother left him
and set a thornless rose upon his grave.

Dust on my fingertips I search
in vain for the soldier's medal
he released on special Sundays
from a war that taught him to be silent.

The abandoned things confirm
the last one to leave
left in a hurry:
the cold fireside, its quiet pressed
against those memories –
the meals my mother made, dreaming by the window
once steeped in thyme and peppermint –
now a backdrop for the shadeless lamp,
and the dusty face of a stopped clock:
a still life on the eating table.

Croaker

The croaking lizard crawls out
from a place it's not supposed to be,
leaping at a moth, transforming me
into a flow of anger.
This room is not big enough
for both of us. The muse
of the next poem whisked away,
the music of the evening raindrops lost,
I realize there's no one else:
the problem is mine alone.

I will it to make a careless move
and coincide with the slap of the broom
as I brace myself, insecticide at hand,
foraging in the fear I must contain.
It's not like the fear that lurks when I see
the gap between platform and moving train;
this fear's worse. Not daring to take
my eyes away, I time its next move –

but, quicker than quicksilver,
after staring at me as if I,
not it, were the son-of-a-bitch,

it disappears behind the glass-framed picture.

The Watertank Revisited

Without the weight of what then seemed important,
I returned to the house under the hill
with its old unfinished watertank, teemed now

with shrubs. From its grave, the ants haul their loot.
Bees, wasps and butterflies are inquiring, romancing.

Its bank slippery as papa's dream,
and scattered with tins whose razor tongues
mimic the sun.

It was my father's job to lift the line in the wind
like a billowing sail, before the clothes swiped the dirt,
to split the wood and start the new foundation.

The watertank: half
-sunk in the soil like a stubborn stare,
is the reason I expected more than his best,
gone to weed, too, now; gathering moss.

I ask myself: what does it matter
that piped water was forestalled?
Besides, what's the past but a rainless day

with dry bush rustling the hill,
and a no-longer-flawed perfection
awaiting another dream to beam from a window,

my father's, mine,
and flow like rain to a tar-glazed water drum planked on flat stones,
guttering in song from a roof,

overflowing to a river no one owns?

A Question of Love

Back when I used to play doctor: I am
passing the house with its blinds fully pulled;
the boarded up window facing the road
nails out the past from what they say love did
to the girl at a city school. Three years
she's been in that room with her diary of hurt.
What stalks her mind robs her of speech.
Like a slate wiped clean, she returns to the bed
that is her fort against the overhang
of whatever fills her mind with its long night.
To hush the shame, no one's invited there.
That house: above eye level from the road,
with whitewashed stones up to the verandah steps
forming two lines from the gate! A hard wind flaps
a nearby breadfruit tree as I pass,
marveling at what the adults deem
might be fruit for a juicy conversation,
blind to the secret in the children's game
of *Thread yuh needle, thread, oh, long, long thread*,
while she, stuck in a world she cannot
leave behind her, lurks in a room
whose curtain never moves in the wind.

The fever with which she danced

Readying herself for what's to come, she turns
to another life, to which she's come to let go,
clap hands and dance, and dream of the place
where a bed overlooks the healing waters' flow,
and a soul wings it over the fields
to whatever lulls her from past conditions,
removing the mask to make peace with grief,
unblinkingly suspending the world elsewhere.

She takes sorrow to where all sense breaks loose
as though possessed, thrown into ecstasy,
singing up the nothingness, free from excuse
in a roomfull of women chanting unknown tongues
while the sole man waves his Bible like a flag of truce,
tip-toeing, prompting the chant, as if to see
into the reaches of their silences
calling forth hallelujahs without apologies.

She takes her respite up St. Peter's Hill
towards the precious fountain, where morning kneels
to admit those things she cannot dismiss,
bearing the moment to a basic blank,
lingering in the shadow of her own free will
where every limb lets go – miming words,
entranced, erasing the onlooker: such was
the fever with which she danced.

That Sunday Morning

She was not begging for forgiveness when she knelt
facing the wall, her head flung back
as if preparing to hold a flashlight to the eyes of Jesus.
Full of argument, raw with energy,
something shouting in her breast flashed clear again
to the August afternoon when the death winds came
to the broken sidewalk that narrows to a lane,
when, after the bullet wrapped itself in silence,
it took the colour from the photo in her purse.

She looked in vain for answers
to what nags her sleep, night after night,
remembering the hour when the sun went down burning
over the yard of scratching chickens, digging
for the words that would tell her all would be well
while the clock ticked to the wrong time.
Talking to Him as if to a next door neighbour
she stood, knowing her anger was not a bluff,
and, with the world still coming to an end,
danced her way up to a victory hallelujah! –
a pitch this poem cannot put into 20 lines.

Pocomania

It could have been how Sister Barclay swung
her skirt and thrashed the tambourine
in the rapture of the unfinished day
quick-stepping under the spirit's influence,

or when Elder Shaw tiptoed
with the Bible in a stranglehold in one hand,
and the Psalm took root,
and the platform trembled under him;

or when he pried the crowd pacing pulpit and pew
and emerged with a string of hallelujahs
and a swift balm, and willed them to be done
with the heartache and the blues.

But something else came over the make-do church
when the bareheaded girl knelt
and rolled in astonishment, and crawled her way
to God across the cold concrete,

and without apparent care coiled loose
from the heartbreak pounding in her head,
her soul stirred in the ecstasy of Pentecost.

Though what did I know at eight
about the bends they crossed
to that shelter from the storm?

Kendal Crash – 1957

*The 1957 train crash at Kendal was the worst rail disaster in Jamaica's history
and the second-worst in the world at that time*

Imagine that September night when the news flashed
to the tenement yard on Sunlight Street
that the excursion train had crashed:
when the man broke down and wept
for his sister torn from her seat
as the song died in her mouth. Imagine

how the tree trunk yielded to the wild burst,
and the door clanged
as the train ploughed into the yam field
near the sleeping town of Kendal; imagine
the priest and pickpocket lending a hand
to someone as the carriage caved in
and the hour sucked the oil from the lamp,

the instant when the train plunged
like a blunt machete through the damp clay
of a moonlit field and the cows broke
into a dismayed gallop,
while rich and poor alike were thrust into the texts
of one another's lives,
jam-packed, trying to hang on
between this world and the next.

Now, year after year, as if to fill
some vacant outpost left by the chill,
the stories clamber back, of the Kendal Ghost
emerging from the stricken stream
to hitchhike into town (or so they say)
then disappear, as in a dream
of morning mist when time came to pay.

DELORES GAUNTLETT

The Balmyard

They knew the yard by the wooden Cross
nailed to the zinc gate around the corner
from my grandmother's house.
There, the Coolie plums
ripened and fell; and there Ms Tasmina,
the childless healer woman, opened her door
to the wild-eyed girl weeping to reverse
a love gone bad,
to the haunted man fleeing the known world
to find a cure
against the makka-tongue of malice and the enemy's rage.

In that yard, the talk of Sunlight Street,
behind the glint of the zinc fence
where it caught and hurled back the sun
the woman was paid
to make the earth tremble
and translate the dreamt messages from the dead,
to lift lives out of unanswerable longing,
crossing herself over an open Bible
to cut the evil spirit
out of the dark caves of her predictions.

One morning, from a peephole in the fence,
I watched the thin trail of smoke
bearing the bald breath of frankincense
like a rumour through her window left ajar
the night before to the shining moon.
I remember the shed from which she brought
the sacrifice while the beheaded chicken pranced,
and how she cried out in three languages, dancing
a stiff quadrille around the current she'd made;
shaken loose by her clients' pain, she spun
around the yard with the fervour
of wasps by whose hive a flame passes,
sprinkling the potion, the oil she drew from fevergrass;
she was the metaphor, a flame held
to the dark of their world,
a leading hand to their lives.

Freeing Her Hands to Clap

... and somehow every Sunday morning
between the kitchen and the eating table,
she redeemed her absence from the village church
with its two pulpits and pipe organ,
while her husband, my father, brought
the noon day how-di-dos on her behalf.
It was the year of the stick swords
and the hoolahoops, when, one day,
under the wide open blue
an eye-popping story wild-fired through
the village vines in overblown proportions
about the 'streets of glory by and by...'
Now, under the essen tree
surrounded by walls of wind
a propped-up streetlight leans
in reverence, as if to pull
power from the lines of heaven
over the valley brimmed with exhaustion.
Dew falls like a blessing
on the congregation, settling like spores,
seeping into her first decision
like the beginning of another end,
and bareheaded she goes
as if to leave all consequences behind, her handkerchief
tucked in her waist,
freeing her hands to clap.

CHRISTIAN CAMPBELL

CHRISTIAN CAMPBELL, of the Bahamas and Trinidad and Tobago, is a poet, cultural critic and journalist. He read English at Balliol College, Oxford as the 2002 Commonwealth Caribbean Rhodes Scholar, and is currently completing a PhD in English at Duke University. His work has appeared in numerous publications, including *Small Axe*, *Wasafiri*, *Indiana Review*, *Caribbean Review of Books*, *Calabash*, *Obsidian III: Black Literature in Review*, *nocturnes (re)view*, *International Poetry Review*, *Atlanta Review* and *The Mays: A Literary Anthology* (an annual collection of the best poetry and short fiction from the universities of Oxford and Cambridge). He is a Cave Canem Poetry Fellow.

Goodman's Bay

Not even a chewed bone,
a used rubber in the seaweed, cut glass
smiling beneath the sand.
We don't see them.

He is my brother.
Our hearts beat the same.
I have bad shoulders,
he has bad knees. We have
given our bodies an atlas.

He breathes softly,
on time, and we talk
very little, the good things, gasping.
I have long legs, one stride
to every two from him.

We run the dusk
at dusk. Everything
is open and live
with silence. All viscera.
God, there is too much
red in the sky.

Making braille in the sand
like this, we feel it in the lower back.
The sinking, the slipping,
all the little slopes and mounds.
We are listening to the body.

Whoever needs to howl
should howl. The warm breath
coming from the sea. The full moon
pulls the tide like a stubborn skirt.

Everything will last.

Children squawk on a swing, flying.
Bahamian children in the night.
The hotels are a glance away.

You feel it when you run
the sand. All of it,
the whole of your body
in the world. The swing
creaks slow, like love
in the morning. God,
the night is so blue.

Man and woman in the dark
water. Ghost and ghost on the seawall.
Someone sews false hair
into a slim girl's dreams.
She does this at night for no good reason.
All this beauty for nothing.

Walking back with our chests
blooming, I taste my own sweat.
There are people dusting off
their feet as if dancing.
We pass a woman in a large,
damp T-shirt, nothing but salt.
We can't see her face,
the smile or the frown, the hard
look of judgment. But the moon
is bareback and blind, and the ground
is an altar of piss and rum, and we know
that somewhere on this split tongue
of stone, someone just died, just finished
making love.

Shells for Sonia Sanchez

You ten, I six, and jujube
now in season. I monkey up
the tree's weak bones and call
down to you, not Wilsonia, that
big-people name. I does call you
Nita. Only them small ocean eyes
that say how you know, I know,
my Mummy know that, boy, jujube
stain don't come out. I'll do most
anything for these plump little suns
and you, even with wasps telling
secret. Is breaktime still and your legs
look skinny under that plaid skirt. You is
give me quarters sometimes, to buy salty.
You's always have your hair in one,
rake and scrape to the side, and if
that don't mean womanish, I don't know
what does. You's the one that start everyone
saying, *That's my prerogative!* You stink
to them teachers but not one child at Xavier's
could test you at singing. I tell people
you's my cousin, but you really the one
that I lend my recorder to longtime so you
wouldn't get licks and you did never forget it.

One time you tell me Santa Claus
fake cause we don't have no chimney
in Nassau and his skin too pink
for this kinda sun and I was sad
because I was hoping for one new bike
so you let me go first in handball. We always
have to pray every morning assembly
Our father who art in heaven
Harold be thy name and I ask you
why Harold so mean to never show
me his art? And the grin how you
answer is keep me glad for days.
I most tall as you, you know, but you
could beat me and plenty boys running
any day, quick as a curly-tail lizard.

Sometimes, when I feel like it, I go up
to people in the schoolyard and point
and say, *What you name?* and you laugh
big as America.

The children don't like me cause
I know my numbers and hard words too
and you say is cause they still is
pee the bed. The children say you
don't have no Mummy and your mouth
too hot. That mouth. Like two piece
of pepper, it stay poke out, a thing
shape for cussing. All neck and pointer
finger, tripping on your tongue. My
Miss Biggety, with your little red self.
Yes you. You who is hum for the trees
always and play ringplay and pinch
the boys that get too fresh. If I did know
you was going with your Daddy to leave
me for true, I would of give you all
my shells and soldier crabs, and even my
new chain. I would of make you learn me
to run fast and sing, if I did know New York
was far-far like the moon.

and for Kerha

Legba

A well-loved lit classic
packed in each bag, and a Harvard
sweatshirt, to match the Pakistani
passport: Iqbal goes first, catching
a flight to France. Then me,
in a tie and soft pants, khaki hat
to keep my mane tame. We chat
clipped and colonial, like our tutors,
grinning out *Oxford* with a nod.
At immigration I put on airs
and styles, let the maleness growl
without teeth. Hold my chest
with untouchable height. All like
a politician, a Sidney Poitier,
an old Bahamian man. I look
only ahead and walk straight-back,
like my grandfather. Speak like he spoke
to foreigners. In his best moods,
he would put on the mouths
of all the Englishmen he'd met,
playing the Queen and how
she gave him his MBE – Pa.
There, reciting and reciting Blake,
until he fell down blank and silent
as any road in Nassau
the morning after junkanoo.

Twilight

Grandmummy mumbles and babbles
over Singh Street, soon gone,
grasps for her grandchildren,
asks their father, *You going to school?*
Everyone whispers, glides past her grayhead,
so as not to trouble the silence
swelling there like a bruise.
But I am walking with her,
back in Granddaddy's big boots,
through chicken mess and mud
to pick ripe pomme cythère.
Back to the twisting spinning kitchen
where her Carib eyes always sang
as she rang a chicken's neck.

Moruga

We going Country they said.
Down Deep South Trinidad
in search of Grandmummy roots.
Come to find crabgrass and troops
of chickens prancing and preening
on Guerrero land like victors of a war.
Foul-smelling turkeys mumbled and trembled
where the wooden house used to stand,
wrinkled and miserable like haggish landlords.
On this road, La Lune Road, Grandmummy
chatter patois with Moruga women,
then listen out for her daddy broken
Spanish flicking at the sea breeze. She bathe
her sandy skin and watch for Venezuela
mountains when the tide low
at the beach just a stone-throw away.
Today I could see Venezuela
and on the shore all the oil-slick corbeaux
quarrelling with their wings.

Anthuriums

Grandmummy's mind left her
and went back to De Country.
Who will talk
to the plants,
comfort the anthuriums,
pick the orchids,
scream from snakes?
I passed through Cochrane Village
last summer: De Ol' House,
home to addicts or abused now,
was overgrown with her life
turned to weeds and crabgrass,
paint flaking fading lonely
like an old hag once beautiful.

Grandmummy followed her mind
back to De Country the other day,
where heart-shaped anthuriums grow
in abundance, and only Mummy could
go down to see her off. Mummy came back
empty-handed and eyes-dry
(no mention of a will),
but she paid her last rites
and gardened more than ever,
potting anthuriums like tombstones,
waiting for the libation from the sky.

Yellow Rooms

In Grenada for the first time, my woman
island, without her, at my writer-friend place
in Morne Jaloux, verandah view

out to bush bush bush
then the Carenage,
we were liming in the kitchen

talking good talk bout books
and freshness over oil-down
cook up by her boxer-boyfriend

when, just so, a bat fly in the place,
flapping wild, nearly buck up
the walls. Everybody duck,

scream with a kind of delight.
It fly fly fly like a madness,
like moth on fire.

The radar off, my friend say.
The damn thing couldn't find
the door it fly in from.

Is a fruit bat right?, I laugh,
I laugh a tremble-laugh.
This creature just come

and mash up all the vibes,
all blind, hairy, all clamour of wings.
Even love, I learn, could be just so,

not meant for this house,
these small, yellow rooms,
a notion, a thing-thing,

old suckblood idea;
who say it could fly in,
dance up in the air and thing;

not a window open again
to chase the thing back out.
Come in like it want stay

for true,
come cause commotion
in I heart.

Repatriation

5th Av. and midnight make my arm tired
of reaching. I am blacker than I think.
Finally a cab, an African driver.
Nigerian, something wicked in me thinks,

but he's Haitian and knows about fleeing.
I will get there fast. Learning that only
sea bounds us, our islands, he churns loose the sing
song of a kweyol-coated tongue. *Do you see*

yourself here for good?, I ask him. All I
catch is: *No. Port-au-Prince. Night. Stars. You know,
la lune.* How the stars dive for the dead, then rise.
How la lune bellies full as Toussaint's hope.

How a New York cab could take me home to sun,
to Nassau, kweyol-pebbles beneath the tongue.

Groove

I never born.
I walk out the water one day,
gleaming and black.
I walk out the water one day,
between Atlantis and The Shack.

Me, I come from conch-songs
and fire and under limbo bars,
wooden monkeys in barrels
where huge dicks spring out,
clapboard houses, goombay,
a raggamuffin's bop, the Ministry
of Tourism. My thing, my thing.

I make of muscle
and rum and straw.
Tiny umbrellas and beads.
And the Bible and Shakespeare
and Africa.

I use to have bubbies,
ripe and handy. I was
a Marketwoman. I was
a Banana Man. I use
to do the fire dance.
I use to run the glass-
bottom boat. I use to rent jet skis
in the kingdom of this beach.

I could fuck
like a goatskin drum.
But the braiders thief my lyrics:
Prettygirl Prettygirl Prettygirl.
I could fuck like a drum.

All day I lift plenty
legs. I prowl. I ride.

Somebody pounce a white gal,
leave her in the bush to dead.

I lift plenty legs. I prowl. I ride.

The black ones believe we
family, but I don't know
them niggers from Adam.

These hotels like mountains.
You have to be barefoot.
You have to dance.
You have to have chest.
When my locks start to sprout,
I will make double.

O I have too much
to want.

America, America. Yes, America.
I run the islands. You come.
Look for me.

On Listening to Shabba While Reading Césaire

for Carolyn and Cecil

... bad   wicked   bad   wicked
badbadbadbad   wicked
& all the purple like skin like bruise like grape like love
       and love and love,
& all the bones get crack and the gold nipples lick,
& all the kinky pubic hair and fantastic abs,
& all the laughter skank away with a necklace of skulls

           I RISE YOU UP

language like embattled iguanas
language like the nectar-crying wound

I walk on hot coals   sweet burning flesh
lianas tremble like the body
melody sliced rectum to throat
the wind makes the sea ejaculate   & again
an old man suck the fish-eye of the moon

there in the crease crevice curve
tongues knifing names on my forearm
I eat out the sap between words

volcano of ganja   bile in the gums   ecstatic spasm of blood
on Saturn's rings bottom to crotch crotch to bottom sliding
& the two mouths together the rugged heart the juice

I would like to say:

fuckery	*funk*	*penumbra*
watermelon	*biggety*	*viscera*
anaphora	*talawa*	*slack*
orgy	*Ogun*	*guerilla*
swagger	*rum*	*flesh*

& let me say:

cerebral	*glammity*	*niggerish*
luminous	*numinous*	*stamina*
arsonist	*backshot*	*agony*
synapse	*maroon*	*gallop*
torrent	*wail*	*rudical*

I would like to say:

. . . . . .

& then:

POWER   POWER   POWER

Don of Guinea   of Gehenna
Gun of golden teeth
O do your jungless science

Rudical

Derek Bennett, killed by police

after Matisse's Icare (Jazz), *1943*

I who born
Thirty-one years
Since *The Windrush* come
Thirty-one years
Life of a man
I who born
Forty-one bullets
Amadou Diallo
Life of a man
Seven kill me
I who born

       & because we suck the neon marrow of the streets
       & because we tote a solar plexus of islands (*for true*)
       & because we yuck out the blue heart of night (*right*)
       & because our heads gather thick as a bloodclot (*teach them*)
       & because we eat out the honey of mad laughter (*everytime*)
       & because we outrun the delirium of streetlights (*ok*)
       & because we are gray bugs scuttling from the lifted rock
       & because & because & &
       & because high street skeets a thousand niggers
       & because my eyehole grows iridescent with the moon
       & because we holler for the bloodclad sun
       & because we mourn the burst testes of the stars
       & because we skank cross rivers of blood

Mine New Cross mine Oldham Notting Hill Bradford Brixton mine too
Nassau Laventille Bridgetown Kingston Britain has branded an x in my flesh
this rolled throat of killings this septic eye this urge of maggotry this seed of
Mars this blasted plot this hurt hissing realm this ogly island this England

LORETTA COLLINS KLOBAH

LORETTA COLLINS KLOBAH is professor of Caribbean literature and creative writing in the English Department of the University of Puerto Rico, Rio Piedras. She has lived in Kingston, Jamaica; London, England, and Toronto. She received her Bachelor's degree in English literature and Masters in English-Creative Writing from California State University, Fresno, her MFA in poetry writing from the University of Iowa Writers' Workshop, and her doctoral degree in English, with an emphasis in Anglophone Caribbean literature, from the University of Iowa. Loretta Collins Klobah currently edits the bilingual literary journal *Tonguas*. Her poetry has been published in such journals as *The Caribbean Writer*, *Poui*, *Cimarron Review*, *TriQuarterly Review*, *Quarterly West*, *Black Warrior Review*, *The Missouri Review*, and *The Antioch Review*. She has also had poetry included in the *Pushcart Prize Anthology*, *TriQuarterly New Writers*, and *How Much Earth: An Anthology of Fresno Poets* (Heyday Books, 2001).

El Velorio, The Wake (1893)

A child's wake in rural Puerto Rico

In Puerto Rico's most famous painting,
El Velorio, a carved pig crucified
on the ceiling beams surveys the crude
beauty of a child's wake, the gray
doll laid out like a bride in its floral wreath
and lace, and *los jíbaros* indulging
in a *baquine* with excesses of spirit and flesh.
The plenitude of green plantains
and dried corn hanging from the rafters
of the wood beam and thatch room
show this to be a home of simple provisions.
A low-slung leather *Taino* chair pushes back
empty from the table, as if the owner
might have risen temporarily to take some
refreshments or air, walking casually through
the open door, past the grazing cattle
and the coffee plantations, and over the hill,
and into the sea. An old African,
head banded, feet bare, and legs crippled,
has his own perspective, looking
down at the baby gathering its halo
of flies. Children brawl on the floor
over calabashes of spilled food
while the babe's mother pours out wine
for the priests. The *cuatro* and *guiro* play on.
Playing cards strewn on the floor
might symbolize the superstitious
faith of the *jíbaro,* the tarot pack,
and bets taken over which neighbor might
provide the next occasion for a country wake.

*****

Did Yashira, playing in the back of a pickup
with two cousins in a rural sector of Corozal,
see the *bala perdida* in flight, the great cosmic bullet
the news media described as 'stray,' as if
it had become lost from its mother, disoriented

and determined to be useful, to penetrate any
flesh in its path? The paper does not mention gun
or culprit, just the anonymous bullet, which
entered Yashira's stomach, exited her back,
and continued on its blind flight.
Six years old, she had appraised
our world wisely enough to tell *la abuela*
'*Me voy a morir*' as she ran to the house
and fell at the threshold. At the home wake,
Osiris Meléndez López, the disconsolate
young mother, brushed her child's hair,
sang and talked to Yashira, rearranging her clothes
for the journey, kissing her goodnight.
This girl, too, was adorned in head wreath and veils.
Juan Ramón, the father, lifted his small bride from the casket,
carrying her to the balcony. In the street, 600 neighbors
who had come to pay respects vomited, ran away,
and cried so that the mourning was heard fifty meters away.
He raged, '*Miren a mi bebé, ella es mi hijita querida,*'
while seven municipal workers laid asphalt
on the driveway where Yashira rode her bicycle.
This visual detail, added to the parent's home
in tribute, will remind them daily of the absence.
Like the *Taino* chair pushed back from the table,
the bicycle will never again seat its owner.
Juan Ramón walked on his knees through wet asphalt
to the funeral service at a nearby church.
We have created a new world where the indiscriminate gun
is always at our backs. From the first murdered *Taino* to now,
the cosmic bullet has been in the air. The carved moon
trots across the sky. Let us rock our babies
to sleep, kissing their hair, rearranging
their night clothes, playing our odds against
carnage, against the stray shot seeking our thresholds.

Going Up, Going Down

for Richard, Miguel, Joel, David and Walter

This is a poem that can't get published – in the Caribbean –
– in Puerto Rico, in St. Croix, in Barbados, in Jamaica,
   in St. Lucia
  I bet you three lotto tickets it can't.

This is a poem that has to roam, has to scavenge,
       has to live in its car, has to live on air,
has to wander the backalleys, has to curl up
     on the steps of your padlocked front door,
has to snatch your straw purse to get a little room
     to crawl into, to breathe in –

Yes, this poem is on the run –
until the Caribbean is ready to greet this poem
   like we meet friends in Puerto Rico, *with a besito* –
  with a saludos, with an embrace.
  See what I mean?

Let's leave orange grove bungalows,
   messy kitchens and plantain rows.
       Excuse me: a grander view of joy
     and liberation in Puerto Rico, a land
     where – as they say in Jamaica – *battybwoys*
     are called *patos* –
     waddling ducks.

     In the elevator, the man's hand brushes
     against a man's jacket.
The red lights of radio towers stub out like cigarettes.
     The men drive through the privacy
     of darkness, humming to Ricky Martin.
     Da da da-da-da da-da, la vida loca.
     The hotel is vacant.
Two scenes: one a still life in the elevator;
one in the realm of action,
     the exhilaration of speed,
     of the roaming car,
     road wind, *reggaeton*, and the hotel

on the horizon.
                A night clerk reads the zodiacs.
        A poui-scented receptionist – *Carmen* –
        books the suite.
All the way
                to the penthouse,
                the man's hand grazes
        the jacket.
        It's raining.

It's like there is a soundtrack to this poem.

    The receptionist casts a seaside gaze –
    she thinks
            it's a spectacle, two men carrying
                    their love for each other
            like a shield – something to tell *Papi*
        about later in bed. The *patos* in room 216.
            She wasn't raised well.

How did these ramblings turn
        homoerotic in the tight space of the elevator, where
            I have put two men bruising accidentally against each other,
        and where I am meditating on their carnal destinations?

Get back, Jack, back
        to where you belong, poem.
Homos don't exist in the Caribbean, poem.
    And get off the beach, poem.

Wrestling boys, my childhood nemeses, now holding
    briefcases under
                their arms, wrestling a cup of coffee.
    Seek the afternoon terraces
            where they will loll in bathing suits,
            warming testicles in the sun.

Is it because corpses lie
                    in little beds of straw in the war zones
        that I must demand
            a little tenderness between men?

That's nasty business, poem. Nastiness.

Is it because I've seen on the evening news
men's legs that had been beaten
    with shovels by the police –
    because they were suspected
    of being
    homosexual
        inna
            Jamaica?

This poem is an eye-witness.
That's why this poem has to be clandestine –
    It is in danger of being stoned –
        Nuh fling rockstone.

            Listen –
    they're in the elevator, trapped between floors.
They have not yet escaped to the other vignette,
the free-wheeling car or
            the seaside tryst.

    Would you like to ask these men anything?

        What do you think of the assault of
            Jane Doe
                in Prospect Park?
    The refugee child who died
        two hours from the border?
In a boat not seaworthy, five miles from the Florida coast?
On the flooded river banks of a Haitian shanty town?
    So much to think about,
    and we have to think about *patos*, poem?

I rub my hands over my eyes. The men do the same.
    Do they pass the time with talk,
    stuck, as they are, in the elevator?
In the grand, airless elevator of the big Caribbean Hotel
    that presses them down, down, down, if they
    try to rise –

    What would you talk about
    if you were stuck in time? Stuck in an elevator
    especially designed for *patos* like you?
    For *battybwoys* like you?

About the International Monetary Fund?

Do these men brag like Tom Arnold
        yukking it up
at the Harley Davidson Cafe, 'I've had more
        pum-pum than ex-President Clinton!
        (and that's
        a lot of pussy!)'?

No, they are better men than that. Sensitive.
    It doesn't matter. They are just men
    trying to love each other.

Would somebody *please* get the censor in here?
    We need to censor this poem, right now!

Let the elevator rest on its proper floor
        and the door slide wide.
Let these men be themselves, to invite love in the way
                that they can.
    Even under the fluorescent glare
    of the elevator, the kiss
        is one of the sweetest they've ever known.

Or perhaps not.
        Why should they satisfy my predilections,
    utopic pleasure, safety, respect, and a Caribbean lullaby?
    A lullaby of One Love?

Novena a La Reina María Lionza

Noche primera

In *las montañas de Sorte*,
in a garden where *Dios* tends his begonias,
yellow-white nosegays for *la reina Maria Lionza*
de Venezuela, she tires of holding a human hip bone
above the stalled motorists of *Yaracuy* –
for fifty barren years, a petrified emblem.
She grows bored of riding a tapir until her pum-pum
rubs raw from the statue's stiff contours. She desires
warm breath from 7th heaven, so a living snake
enters the iron helix encircling her ankles.
His copper coils clench and tug until *la reina*
feels sensation again. She arches back, nipples
pointed at the stars, a deity of *la naturaleza*
craving the diamond pinpricks of space.
Damballa eases into her until she pants, jaguar
in heat, and her casing splits. Concrete
and steel torso shattered, *Maria Lionza* slips free.
Papers vow it's a celestial sign that President Chavez will fail.
But she just has to wheel away, above *la autopista*
deadlocked around her feet, an obsidian Anaconda.
She has to seek out what is still grass-green
in the cemetery cities of her *El Dorado*
and our islands, on earth's cement crust.

Noche segunda

In *Yabocoa*,
the winds catch a woman bathing in the storm.
Imagine, she just wanted a body-slam bracer of wet wind.
She wanted to be deluged and rocked in air alive all around her –
like those men who lash themselves to palm trees.
She wanted *Huracán* to breathe life into a manikin.
Instead gales coil her zinc roof into a tight watch spring
and slingshot her hammock and bikini-body into the sky.
In the *periodico*, we see her deflated, buckled corpse
elegantly sprawled in her neighbor's gutter.
We see rows of prostrate plantains that spread out

their green hands over the flood waters like
devastated supplicants praying in a mosque.
What that news story does to me – a rag-doll woman
catapulted from her hammock into god's lungs!
Maria Lionza, Storm Jeanne is not done with us yet.

Noche tercera

In Puerto Rico, after
we have dreaded the spiral galaxies of hurricanes
traveling towards us at light speed in web satellite shots,
after the evil eyes of the storms have seen all that they want
of our island, we measure the nights in candle-hours.
'Todo Puerto Rico queda sin luz y 500 mil abonados sin agua.'
Yes, we are used to it. Still, each psyche is flooded.
In these weeks we hear radio news from our sister islands.
The bay and marina of red-roofed Grenada!
A ten-year-old girl drowned in Jamaica.
Gonaives, Haiti – trees used up for fuel and coal-pots,
nothing much to anchor soil when floodwaters came.
Families stranded in trees with no food. Two children
on a porch, their faces covered with cloths. The man in a flowered
dress watched his children and neighbors swept away.
The student begged soldiers to remove eleven bodies
floating in his house, four brothers and a sister.
When we may leave our homes, neighbors laugh
about the babies made in the storm: what else was there to do
sin luz? Babies made, babies lost in the storms.

Immaculate noche cuarta

The *ciclón* remains, rumbling in the belly of a great boa constrictor.
The boa spends his mornings bumping the attic boards of a *casita*.
He passes secret nights smudging moist trails on the bedsheets
of a thirty-two-year-old girl who cannot speak.

Night after night after night, the great snake presses
his shape into her bedcovers, curling around the hot feet
of a woman with a child's mind and no speech.

Let us say that this woman lives with her mother
in the shadows of the green *mogotes*, the flooded hills
that conceal whatever creatures that still survive
the asphalt, strip malls, and jump-up election caravans.

In other *casitas* belligerent boas, made nervous refugees
by floodwaters, are cornered in bathrooms, bagged up
and hauled off. But this one goes undiscovered for days.
Imagine it, the nightly encounter. She can't talk.

And if the dumb beauty rides a tapir in the dark room,
or raises her own hip bones to the sky, or bathes
in nosegays of sun-white flowers, or sits
in simple contemplation of the massive snake,
her mother remains insensate to these developments.

For days the daughter studies the snake. He doesn't abduct her.
He doesn't consume her, burst, and birth her out,
a yellow African, *Indio*, Spanish water goddess
wearing jade pendant and pearls. He does not have articulate
human speech. He is silent, or hisses, or climbs trees.

Our woman listens to Damballa, but she does not become
la reina María Lionza de Puerto Rico y Venezuela.
Her figurine will not be sold at *Botánica Santa Barbara.*
A benevolent *lwa* cannot carry messages to his children
through speech, *y una chica* cannot transmit his message.

Noche quinta

     City of enemy hands,
City unconcerned with piety and purity of heart,
City that forgets its collapsed bridges *y arboles caídos*,
City that forgets children sucked into floodwaters,
City that uproots, designs, executes, emits,
City of daily *lucha*, nightly struggle,
I had the desire today to lie on my back
under a turpentine tree on the ant-filled grass.
I wanted to see the wet leaves moving and the light.
I wanted succulent heat on my forehead and breeze.
I wanted to go to *el jardín botánico*
and lie down near green water and turtles,

let the sun create red hibiscus flowers on my inner eyelids.
But I didn't. The city kept beating me with its chiseled fists.
Can't I just lie down in my business suit under a tree?
When the light comes down in this city,
it does not illuminate
anything but leaves.

Noche sexta

What María Lionza said:
Follow the road in the belly of a snake,
through marsh saw-grass and Job's tears,
fragrant swamp flatsedge and *Caña brava*,
down to the *manglar*. Fiddler crabs
trace musical staffs along the salt flats –
violinistas and glazed flats the color of sandstone.
Taste salt-crystal leaves of the black mangroves.
Colonies of red mangroves dip the dense brushes
of their aerial roots into the sea.
When the bright, reflective surface of the *laguna*
photographs the mangroves and clouds perfectly,
it makes a mirror I do not want to stop gazing into.

Noche séptima

A mute girl and a disoriented snake
made me think of María Lionza; made
me search music stores for the song
by Rubén Blades and Willie Colón;
made me listen to it on the car CD player
until my daughter could sing it;
made me walk Río Piedras, from
botánica to *botánica*, looking fruitlessly
for a figurine of *La Reina María Lionza*;
made me sleeplessly surf the internet,
where I found that her statue in Venezuela
had fallen apart that same week.
I did not find you, *diosa de la naturaleza*,
but you are the running vine binding my ankle.
Help me to shed my dead skin.
One *botánica* owner found a sheaf of prayers,

a *novena* to *La Reina María Lionza.*
He could only talk about the tropical depressions
still forming off of Africa.

Noche octava

We open the earth
with a little red shovel.
Red clay and worms.
A clay crater in *la tierra.*
She holds the tree
close to her belly,
it's roots paper-bagged.
An *Emajaguilla* tree,
Spanish Cork, its already
dense crown of leaves
deeply heart shaped,
verde oscuro brillante.
Yellow-purple flame
flowers will bell out later.
My daughter and I
learn how to midwife
a tree of green hearts.
Un hoyo dos veces mas
ancho y el mismo profundidad
del envase de las raices.
We stake it and tie it.
We give it water.
It looks good to us.
Its trunk is a straight spine.
We have taken the time.
We have platforms of red clay
on our shoes.
She says, 'I love this tree.'

Noche novena

An eggshell of the serpent, *la cuidad de San Juan.*
I want to chip it and crack it.
I've been inside a long time.
I want to star-gaze on the boardwalk of *Piñones.*
Daughter, look at the great storm brewing
now and always on Jupiter. Swing the scope
wide to our hills, to the snake-furrows
and side-winding valleys
of Earth where the birds flit up
and become stars. Dark now.
No rainbow after these storms.
Let us move away from the city's thunder.
Don't ask me for mall-debris
that a month later swells landfills.
Ask me for this: our night breaths sketching
vectors between sea and Orion's red shoulder,
our bodies revived by surf boom.
We'll raise miniature goats –
you'll feel their lips
nuzzling grains in your palm.
I want to grow you in a green-heart place
above the flood plains,
where after our terrible storms,
only roosters cry,
and, if we are blessed,
the serene snake
visits our bedrooms.

The Twelve-Foot Neon Woman on Top of Marla's Exotik Pleasure Palace Speaks of Papayas, Hurricanes, and Wakes

Look, with that scaffold up my back,
I was feeling Christ-like, like the stone Xavior
on the rock pinnacles of Río de Janeiro.
Felt like conducting the bloody symphony
of carnival in Río's Sambodrome, or stalking
through the streets like Oya, orisha of whirlwinds
and cemeteries. Felt like flying to Guadeloupe,
Point-á-Pitre, where Kweyol rap booms through
the graveyards. Felt like landing on the black and white
checkerboard crypts of Morne-à-l'Eau.
Felt like it would free me from mourning you.
Felt like tasting of salt, and reggae, and rude boys.
Felt like sunning myself on the walls of the Fortaleza.
Felt like stretching my electric legs.
Felt like having daughters, big round brown
ones, who dance bomba in green skirts
and splash away from the crystalline jellyfish
and darting diamond angels of Aguadilla and Luquillo.
Felt like never cooking again, especially for you.
Felt like eating salty alcapurias con yucca y guineo.
Felt like banishing the tired crone in me, the one
begging Obatala for healing, patience, and wisdom.
Felt like riding a Shango train song all the way home,
letting the blues of it, and the R&B of it, and the funk
of it, and the beguine of it, and the mento of it,
and the quadrille of it rattle my hip bones to heaven.
Felt like starting a fire. Felt like starting a really big
conflagration to burn the urban plantation.
Felt like dressing in glass beads and silver.
Felt like tracking hurricanes, felt like drinking
tea of anise and lime peels. Felt like taking a bush bath
to cure the you in me. Felt like playing the cuatro
at a wake. Felt the Chupacabra in me rising –
Puerto Rican, blood-sucking souciant.
Check it out. Nine thousand websites
have reported sightings of me, a creature
who terrifies Paso Finos in the fields, drains

the blood of fowls, ram goats, and pigs without
tearing flesh. The spines ridging my back
are raised. See the warning?
So I got down from the scaffold, baby,
and I switched off my neon tits, blink, blink...
When you call, I'm not home. I'm listening
to Stevie Wonder. I'm listening to my daughter
listen to Sister Carol who chats, singjay stylee,
about the natural jacuzzi I have in my rainforest backyard.
The flamboyant flames, the papayas are lush,
and neighbors give me star fruit and poma rosa by the bag.
Why did I let you bring me down, Papi?
Mamma and daddy only taught me how to sing
the blues; you taught me how to write them.
My only tears are for history, now.
Felt like wearing a cornflower blue dress, hem
trailing the water I walk on, tossing stars
into sea foam. Felt like weaving
Pennyroyale into my hair. Felt like writing
my son and daughter all my love songs –
each one ending with the words 'fyah burn.'

By the Waters of St. Lucia

... and the dispossessed/ said the rosary of islands for three hundred years
Derek Walcott, *The Star Apple Kingdom*

The library is locked, but behind the grillwork windows
slant antique volumes carried from Rome to this island enclave
where iguanas scrawl their own missals in moonlight and sand.

The Benedictine Sisters of St. Lucia let my daughter ride
their skirts, work habits of canvas, old sails of tallship Brig Unicorn
cut to size; she tugs their skirts from kitchen to stone altar,
absorbing the blaze of hearth, of hand-baked guava tarts,
and sun-hallowed light of the stained-glass St. Scholastica.

From the greenweb of bush forest, the clearing of the monastery
offers a woman space to rest near the shade of prickly pear,
pumpkin vines, and stone fish pond. Offers a small girl room
to tilt her face to rain, trouble Sammy the guard dog, and spy
sailboats and puddle-hoppers descending on Castries.

We do what others do, take a tour to Choiseul, Vieux Fort,
Soufrière, the volcano's bilging sulfur, boiling dark water.
The driver dismisses Walcott's allusion to the conical Piton
mountains as Helen's serene breasts. *'A poet has his own way of seeing,*
the Pitons are miles apart.'
We cross the island, through villages
of wooden houses open to the weather, where, says the guide,
politicians appear before elections and then vanish, *'Work? What work?'*
In Soufrière, we see the government-built lockers
for the fishermen, salt-rusted zinc and screen-wire lean-tos.

In Anse la Raye, where street vendors sell blackened corn and whelks,
and country & western music plays, we eat a seasoned fish,
wrapped in foil and stewed in its juices, and roasted breadfruit.
For me, Walcott's lines, poorly remembered, filter rain forests
and fishing villages, Rastafari and school girls along the narrow road.

My daughter loves the nuns. She watches them halve oranges
and squeeze the juice into a pitcher. I ask Sister Emmanuela
nothing about the massacred Irish nun, the damaged church,
or the men who styled themselves as Rasta and burned Babylon.
Raised Protestant and lapsed early into godlessness,

attracted more to Rasta reasonings than Rome's *kyrie eleison*,
who am I to balance anyone's heart against a feather?

Women from two islands far from Zion, we talk
while a three-year-old girl runs everywhere,
making a Sister look at her reflection in a gold doorknob,
leaving a naked, armless Barbie doll in the sanctuary.

When we go home to Puerto Rico, everyday a young man
will recite his litany at our window, *'Missy, some change'*
for food, medicine, or *drogas*. He will show his one bad foot,
where bloody lesions boil into small volcanic mountains.
I used to want to ask where his mother was.
Now some days I give change, some I don't.
After days of downpour in the wet season,
he will greet me on the corner, a foil windshield
protector held over his head like a small galvanized roof.
'Missy, how do I look?' Like so many other
street people in advanced stages of *SIDA*.

He will die one day in the street. He will sleep
on the steps of El Ladrillo Bar and wake
to pains that rock him. All morning he will rock himself
on the sidewalk as my neighbors and I do nothing.
Someone will finally call the police. They will arrive
on bicycles and then scribble notes on clipboards
while he rocks and tucks into a fetal ball.
Before he is cleared from the street,
an *El Nuevo Día* photographer might snap
his feet soles curled together like a sleeping infant's.

My daughter tells a Sister that she wants
to be a mermaid with a long tail. On the plane, she will
see mermaids in cloud nets cast by Martinique,
and the tourists in the seat behind us will ask of saintly islands,
from St. Vincent to St. Thomas, *'Is that Puerto Rico?*
It looks more affluent than St. Lucia from the air.'
On descent, my daughter and I will glimpse our street
of red *flamboyán* trees, where a bearded man
kicks a rosary of fallen flame blossoms.
Scarlet, purple, and blood-black sores bloom on his legs.
Sunset, he walks from window to window,
hailing each María to bestow upon him a small grace.
For a short time, we will be above it all.

Two Women Chatting by the Sea (1856)

Before Camille Pissarro left St. Thomas island
to become a father of French Impressionism,
he studied women bending to their chores,
washerwomen and water carriers, African
women of the Danish West Indies, sketched barefoot
and rooted to their tasks of lifting and cleansing
at the stone well. He had not yet added
the yellow hatchworks of light that fall
brilliantly on brightly garbed peasants
laboring in the patchwork grain fields of Pontoise.
He drafted the curvature and hoist,
the spine's taut response to the weight
of things that must be carried, the rounded
shoulders of a woman gathering bundles low
to the ground and her erect exactitude in balancing
loaded trays upon her head. One penciled
study of a mule traces the heavy neck
swaying low and legs hobbled closely together
so that the joints bend awkwardly inward.
A workbench must have stood nearby,
but Pissarro drew only a solitary vise.
The mule and the steel clamp on a white
page beg for the viewer to interpret symbolically
the mule's burdens and constraints. Later landscapes
burn with the steady effort of leverage,
the belabored body bowing in dashes of sunlight.
Field dancers galloping in hand-clasping roundels
under a dusk sky move with the cadence of labor.
Women apple pickers and gleaners stay in the fields
until the gold light turns indigo and then deep blue.
By the time Pissarro left St. Thomas, slave laborers
in St. Croix were rising up against their masters.
The world was starting to lose its edges,
its clear definitions of color and order.
Even for the European bourgeoisie painted at leisure
in the newly wrought light of the Impressionists,
nothing was certain. Whirling winds in Van Gogh's
night sky were the winds of change,
not the troubled dreams of a mystic painter
alone, but the churning of a world

changing its human wobble to the rhythms
of Karl Marx, Frantz Fanon, and C.L.R. James.
The son of a union unrecognized by Jewish elders,
with a Sephardic Jewish haberdasher
born in Bordeaux as a father and a mother
about whom little is known, except that she haled
from the island of Dominica, Pissarro schooled
with the illegitimate heirs of the Danish plantations
and black children at a primary run by Moravian pastors.
As were many middle-class children of the islands,
Pissarro was later sent away to boarding school in France.
We can blame him for missing the opportunity
of painting the post-slavery islands into art history,
of fleeing to peasant villages where he could escape
disdainful glances of the African women he drew
and the sellers and buyers at West Indian market squares.
In the open markets of France, people sorted cabbages
and butchered pork without thinking of the far colonies
and their freed darker-skinned counterparts toting
vegetables and calling customers in creole songs.
How tedious it must have been, though, for a young man,
returned from school to labor in his father's haberdashery.
He inventoried the staples sold to the ladies
of Charlotte Amalie and dusted shelves.
At twenty-two, he got away, sailing with painter
Fritz Melbye to Caracas, Venezuela, and then France,
where he and other vagabond artists and anarchists
noticed how the light was gradually changing.
He came to love the detailed drawings by
the Japanese artist Katsushika Kousai,
prints of artisans, the net menders,
wheelwrights, and grain grinders bowed
to their work. He began to disdain the monied classes.
In one of Pissarro's few completed paintings
depicting daily life in St. Thomas,
two women pause on a wheel-ridged path
by the sea, their backs to the whitewashed hillcrest
and the foggy surf break, where a miniature party
leisurely searches for seashells or prepares
for a Sunday feast at the water's edge.
A lady must lead the distant gathering
since someone lifts a black umbrella,
the sort carried in the Caribbean to protect fair

complexions from the salted surf bite and sun glare.
In the foreground, the African women
brace their loads, one wields a larder basket,
one an amply laden headtray draped in white
lace linen. Passing upon the path,
they have stopped out of hearing distance
from both the painter and the small party
that gazes out to sea where no Danish prows
perturb the waves. Both wear dresses flounced
with extra yardage at the waist. The woman
in white is collared by an orange and red scarf
caught in the breeze. It could lift her up
suddenly into the air and over the hill
and away to wherever she wants to go
if it were not for the ballast of the headtray
anchoring her to the path. Their conversation
belongs to themselves alone.

SHARA McCALLUM

SHARA McCALLUM is originally from Jamaica, and now lives in the United States, where she teaches and directs the Stadler Center for Poetry at Bucknell University, Pennsylvania. She is also on the faculty of the Stonecoast Low Residency MFA programme. She is the author of two books of poems, *Song of Thieves* (2003) and *The Water Between Us*, the winner of the 1998 Agnes Lynch Starrett Poetry Prize (1999), both published by the University of Pittsburgh Press. She has been the recipient of an Academy of American Poets Prize, a Tennessee Individual Artist Grant, and a grant from the Barbara Deming Memorial Fund. Shara McCallum's poems and personal essays have appeared in such journals as *The Antioch Review*, *Callaloo*, *Creative Nonfiction*, *The Iowa Review*, *Ploughshares*, *Virginia Quarterly Review* and *Witness*.

Now the Guitar Begins

1   Last Song

There is a field with no light.
Not the faint shimmer of stars,
not the sliver of a moon.
This night, there is a man
walking guitarless in the grass,
no song in his pocket,
no tune on his tongue. Empty
your voice for him,
it will be no use.
In this field, there is this man
and not even a hint of wind
can stir the tall weeds
through which he moves.
He will lie down, smell
the earth fresh from rain.
He will listen to crickets,
a music he cannot understand.
He will close his eyes.
He will sleep.
He will not get up.

2   A Story

My father thought he was the devil
so he ate an entire chocolate cake –

one my mother had baked –
icing and all, not a crumb left

on the plate. *You must have known,*
he said to my mother. *The voices*

must have instructed you.
A devil's food cake, all for me.

My father thought
he was a god

so he took a broom
to my mother's head

until blood bloomed
on her face, until

her elbow splintered and he saw
what he had done

and it was not good.
Then my father wept.

The voices were a gift.
How could he explain

to one not privileged
to such knowledge?

I walk and freeze midstep
and must not move at all,

he told my mother,
or the earth will fly apart.

To keep things whole –
don't you see Migdee? –

I must stay still.
Perfectly still.

3 Fate

Nights, my father's voice trawls
the surface of my skin, his rasping
insistent across the gorge of time.

Days, the sound of the sea
is the sound of wind
in the trees, is the sound

of my longing for an end
to this searching
everywhere for his face.

Under the shadow of the banyan,
I see our lives revealed.
Dark and light twinned

within each cell,
I was born with a truth
even he could not bear.

And for that, I have been cast out.
Beloved before any other,
I was once the brightest star

in his heavens.
How does he think –
now exiled – I can live?

4 Electroshock

Imagine it is only light
entering your skin.
Imagine you are submitting
to God's will.

Imagine your body
a fan opening and closing,
fingers like tendrils of seaweed
in an aquamarine dream.

Ask me what it feels like
to break down to your smallest parts,
to feel yourself reduced
to a wind-spray of salt.

Ask me what it means to be
nothing, to be less than even that.
Ask me and I will tell you
because I was there

when the voice filled
the reverberating air,
the moment before it dimmed
and then was gone.

5 Fugue

I

Lemons relinquish their scent
to the breeze.
In the garden, if I could
hold the guitar, its music
thrumming in my hands.
All day the sun
sifts through the trees.

II

Veins are black birds
clawing beneath skin.
Doctor says to swallow
the pinks, yellows, reds.
But once I heard Jesus
speaking in my voice.

III

Words are water
slipping through my hands.
Where is Migdalia? So grey,
so blue, her eyes,
like the sky, like the moon
even now
just before dark.

6 The Call

At the end of his life, my father stood
at a pay phone in the rain, crying
and calling my mother's name
into the hollow cup of the receiver
mashed close to his mouth,
hair matted, eyes roaming
the distant fields, vacant
without sound. Light
from somewhere beyond the trees

beckoned and he ceased to hear,
only saw a flickering
of birds, angels rustling their wings.

7 Interlude

You are dead
so I wallpaper this room:
white roses for the sound
of your last breath.

I am a flower blooming
out of season: poinsettia in spring,
leaves burning red
long after the last thaw.

In winter, nothing blooms
beneath snow: my breath
on this pane of glass,
white petals of ice.

Death is a chrysanthemum,
the sound of earth covering its face.
You are dead
And I have no breath

enough to call you back:
hyacinth, dahlia, ambrosia,
Alastair, father, son.
The dead have many names

but carry to the grave
the sound of each one.

8 Genesis

In my belly grows a tree.
From that tree, there is light.
In that light, a place
where you are again a son.

Alastair, do branches of this tree
break under the weight
of your shame? Do its leaves
rupture into wounds?

As it was in the beginning
so shall it be in the end,
the body turning back
on itself:

in fear, in love.

9   Music Not Meant for Music's Cage

When I hear you again
fifteen years have passed.
Your throat has long since closed.
I am no longer a bird in your palm.

On this road from Mobay to Negril,
you appear when called: returned
for a moment by the miracle
of recorded song. But after this time

of waiting, I do not recognise your voice,
these words, this song of a thousand birds,
each beating its wings
against the scaffold of my ribs.

10   Coda

So it has come to this:
You have become symbol
of all I cannot name.

Once, I imagined you
a bird, a heron wading through salt water
marshes, mangroves rooted in sand.

A flush of fish in another dream,
your colours brighter than the possibility
of all reefs.

Or a house on stilts,
out in the shallows of the sea,
whittled by salt, wind, and rain.

The truth I hate to admit
even now is this: I was a child
and you, a man, unreachable

from where I stood
gazing up at your face,
a night with few stars.

I did not know you,
then nor now, anymore
it seems than you knew yourself.

Left with the worst of possible choices –
forgive me –
I made you up.

11 The Flamboyant

The child runs and sand
flaps up in her wake.

He will branch into blossoms
of salt and light.

She does not look back, pressing
her ear to the memory of skin.

His arms grow into the earth,
fingers root in the soil.

Petals rain onto her face.
Sunlight splinters through leaves.

His chest explodes into flowers
of the flame tree, slivers of fire.

What I'm Telling You

My father played music. He played a guitar and sang. My father
recorded his songs in the same studio where Bob Marley played
with his band. And if you know who Bob is and are thinking
'One Love,' dreadlocks, ganja, *hey mon*, then you are straying
from the centre of this poem, which is the recording studio
where I slept on the floor while my father sang and strummed
his guitar. And where Bob, who was only a brother in Twelve
Tribes to me at four or five, said to the man who called me *whitey
gal* that I was not, that I was a daughter of Israel, that I was
Stair's child. That same Bob who you've seen shaking his natty
dreads and jumping up and down; that same man with the
voice of liquid black gold became a legend in my mind too at
four or five as a record somewhere in a studio in Jamaica started
to spin.

from *jack mandoora me no choose none*

3

in some stories   you have no choice
                  you can't remember
                          the truth
    it is not possible
           to go back
              to uncover
                        cause
       discover
            who really
                 is at fault

so you have to say
           is anancy do it
     you have to say
         an evil witch   cast a spell
                forget
                  she was overlooked
                  not considered to bless
                     the child
you have to remember   only
         the spinning wheel
         drops of blood
         light   leading the child   from her parents

then   it is not
        the mother
        the father
            it is only a story
       you are trying
           to remember
              (to forget)

4

if yu wan fi know why
    mongoose nyam up chicken only
    why im so scarnful a meat

listen carefully:

one time   farmer give anancy and mongoose   dem pick a two rope
   fi choose   one a im animal dem
            an anancy rope lead im to de fowl

     anancy   being anancy   was vex
       afta im mek   such a poor choice
           an tink up a plan   fi spite mongoose
 (forget   se im spose to be frien to mongoose)

              tiefin de cow
         mongoose chose
       anancy cut off de tail
      id it inna de groun   (wid only one en stickin out)
        an tell mongoose   im cow walk down dere
   never fi come back
           (same time now offerin im chicken
           to mongoose
           fi mek imself look good)

    now mongoose will only eat fowl meat

   no matter   if you were to tell him
              the truth
 take him back   show him   how anancy deceived him
             it wouldn't matter

  to this day   mongoose   will not hear you
    he will not forgive
      that cow for deserting him

            some say
            it is just a matter of taste
            that mongoose grew

  unaccustomed to certain flesh

but i say   is anancy cause it   is anancy mek it   it is anancy
             who started it

      jack mandoora me no choose none

The tragedy of the mermaid

is not that she must leave her home
but that she must cast off her flesh.
To love, she must lose scales as a child
relinquishes dolls to youth;
she must hide the shells
she plants under her tongue,
culling her dreams;
she must stop the tide rising
in her breath each night;
she must stem the scent of salt
seeping from her skin.
Touching her shrivelled face,
she must not feel an ocean
falling from her eyes.

What the Oracle Said

You will leave your home:
nothing will hold you.
You will wear dresses of gold; skins
of silver, copper, and bronze.
The sky above you will shift in meaning
each time you think you understand.
You will spend a lifetime chipping away layers
of flesh. The shadow of your scales
will always remain. You will be marked
by sulphur and salt.
You will bathe endlessly in clear streams and fail
to rid yourself of that scent.
Your feet will never be your own.
Stone will be your path.
Storms will follow in your wake,
destroying all those who take you in.
You will desert your children
kill your lovers and devour their flesh.
You will love no one
but the wind and ache of your bones.
Neither will love you in return.
With age, your hair will grow matted and dull,
your skin will gape and hang in long folds,
your eyes will cease to shine.
But nothing will be enough.
The sea will never take you back.

Dove

Imagine if you could have either *cherry* or *stove*,
but not both; if the sound of rain
would not answer to its name: *tap, tap, pitter pat.*
If one morning you woke and had to say *dove*,
not *love*, and mean it. If this went on
all through the day and night and into early dawn –
this calling of the world and all its parts
a single word: your cat's meow,
the kumquat freshly washed at the sink,
the milk bottle in the fridge, swallows
outside listing on the wind, the grey slant
of falling rain, a lover's hand grazing your neck.

Election Days

There are days so long the sun
seems always overhead, a hefted
medallion hanging in the sky.
They sit in the market,
gathering like flies on fruit, linger in dust
kicked up on roads scorched by drought.
They lie on the base of the neck
like beads of sweat stalling on skin.

These are the days in a country's life
when the air is so still it collects
in folds, drapes itself
through the nostrils of young and old;
when the air is weighted
with something approximating hope.

Dear History

Believe me when I tell you
I did not know her name

but remember the colour of her dress:
red, like my own school uniform.

I did not know death could come to a girl
walking home, stick in hand,

tracing circles in the dirt,
singing as she went along.

I did not know death
would find someone

for wearing the wrong colour smock
in the wrong part of town.

My parents spoke in hushed tones,
but I heard the story of her body

dragged from street to gully,
left sullied in semen and blood.

I heard the song she sang,
the one I wish I could sing now.

Truth is, I was that girl.
Truth is, I was never there.

Mother and Child

Forgive the artist this scene.
She was taught to paint what she can see.
Forgive the sun that shone that day,
light glistening off the mother's nutmeg skin,
finding beauty in the most improbable places.
Forgive the dead child in her arms
for running into the path of a bullet
as if running after the tail of a kite.
Forgive the brushes. Forgive the paint.
Forgive the wide *o* of the mother's mouth
the wail that will always remain
lodged in her throat.
Forgive the silence of the canvas
like the silence of God
waiting to be filled with sound.

TANYA SHIRLEY

TANYA SHIRLEY is a graduate student and teacher in the Department of Literatures in English at the University of the West Indies, Mona campus. She earned an MFA in Creative Writing from the University of Maryland in the United States. Her work has appeared in *Small Axe* and *The Caribbean Writer*, and she received an International Publication Prize from *Atlanta Review* in 2005. She is a Cave Canem Fellow and a past participant in *Callaloo* Creative Writing Workshops.

Guinep

To eat a guinep you must first crack the skin

I am always aware of my mouth and how easily things slip in

There is a myth that follows the fruit like an after-bite

The child who swallows the seed must be turned upside down

I am always aware of my legs on the ground

I am aware that my angle on the ceiling depends on the eating of a fruit

There is no reason to claim control: your mouth could kill you

Clamp down like the first crack of skin or your earliest attempt at speaking

The seed is guarded by a glutinous flesh tempting enough to be called sweet

You are left hanging by the feet and haunted by the fruit

It is not the same if you destroy the heart of the enemy

It is how you hold your mouth

Out of Body

That wasn't love: that was
you unravelling quietly
on the backseat,

lying back thinking
you never dreamed
phallic was this big.

You skipped
your favourite:
stew peas and rice,

for this?
You should eat something
before you take in

too much air. Fill yourself
with yellow and gold
or the sounds of rain

falling out of a movie
you remember watching
when no one was on top of you.

You move your right hand
down the slope of back.
Jesus!

You've never prayed like this,
for flesh and flood.
You've found a village.

This place is your own:
the smell of you
like damp earth and curry.

What sex are we
twined like bamboo stalks
in a farmer's hands,

journeying to the sound
of a car engine?
Me, somewhere on a gravelled road.

Sunday Ritual

I would buy a bottle of cheap red wine
keep it on the dining room table
like a fine sculptured statue,
until Sunday came
when I would pour its contents,
pretending it was the ocean
fermented to red,
into a fake crystal glass and drink
glass after glass after glass
until all that remained was the bloody bottom of the sea.

Sundays were always hard on my heart, easy on my pen.
I was never a poet then, just a girl
longing to be home
in the presence of my mother's complaining:
'Why you young people don't like church? Eh?
The old choir so old that all of them combined
don't have a full mouth of teeth.'

To be home again,
I would give the old people all my teeth.
Hand-wrap them and deliver them at the altar
like a mash-mouth virgin.
Here, my mouth is full but my tongue is numb.
Just for remembrance, I talk patwa to the furniture.
The brown couch is a broad back woman
with a basket of fruits on her head
and three sons at home sleeping.
The coffee table is always my father,
stained in the middle and most days left unpolished.
The frigid snow stuck to the patio door
is the ripe belly of a coconut I speak to while eating.

Here, you must turn food into language.
Cook tin ackee and fresh codfish
until the aroma says,
'Mawning, how you do? Long time no see.'

On Sundays the heater is set to sunshine
and with my breasts drooping in a floral cotton wrap,
sweat trickling past my navel into my communion cup,
I curl up and die another day in this place.

The Life Left Behind

This time when she left you
she didn't take the children

nor the revealing dresses,
not even the deep purple one with the rose,
you had given her last Christmas,
instead of the usual household appliance
or your disappearance,

not even her lipsticks with their stale smell
nor the blue and grey eye shadows that made her dream.

She saw in the faces of her children
the moments they were conceived,

especially Lutie, whose brown eyes
always made her feel guilty
for staying and for leaving.

She left a message on the stationery
your grandfather had given as a wedding gift.
Her words would never let you know
she was leaving
this time for good.

So, she left you
little drawings of birds
with their beaks so pointed
you thought they were carrying
knives in their mouths.

The Music Man

for Kwame Dawes

I

A man strums his guitar so hard it bleeds.
Washed in his blood we swoon and sway like cane.
Converts, we rise to meet his tremulous voice,
to break bread at the river's mouth, to harvest
ourselves in each soil-soaked note.
We lay our crosses down in the bed of his bellows.
The pluck of each string, a sermon of sound uprooting,
uprooting a past of lay-me-down, tears anchored to salt.

II

He holds the last note in the cup of his mouth.
Sip by sip we are saved. His fingers quiver over
a single string until no one is left standing.
On our bellies we crawl like crabs to his feet.
Let us live in your kingdom. But like Anancy
he shifts shape and walks out the room – a man.

She Who Sleeps With Bones

I've now become an unwilling seer
who will grow old and appear
to be a shaman to the unbelievers;
a tattered woman who smells
of feculent potions.

My mother could see from the back
of her head, the enemy approaching.
She deciphered the codes of dreams
and scared children with her prophecies
of parents drowning.

I decided long ago I would never
grow into her. To be sure, I slept
with one eye open and never ate past six
in the evening: full belly causes dreaming.
Dreams give deep meaning.
But still the curse chose me
and I see:

Water means longing;
the long buried relative visiting the living
is old dead come for new dead;
lizards are enemies or pregnancy;
a wedding is a death; a funeral a birth;
a fish means there'll soon be a baby;
shit is money and prosperity.

Already I know too much.
It will kill me to give this up.
Dead people breathe down my neck.
Their bones creak when I roll over in my sleep.
Last week my husband left.
I do not remember his name or how we met.
I belong to the land of my mother and look behind.

My name

for Helena

I said, 'Hello, my name is Tanya.'

She laughed the bend backwards
show your teeth and throat laugh.

She said, 'I dig up Tania outside.
Go down on my knees
dig my hands into the earth
and pull Tania out. Cook it in soup
with Irish potato and dumpling.
It's like a yam, you see.
So you never knew
you were ground provision?'

No, but I always knew
I was deeper
than this life I'm living.

Now, I keep thinking
what it means to be one
with the earth, to face each day
with the threat of being eaten.

Cancer (Part I)

It is hard staring stench in the face
when you know he doesn't belong
in the cavern of a woman who reared roses
and brought a mango tree all the way from Jamaica
for the neighbours who couldn't afford to travel.

Luna, slice of the moon, daughter of Miss Iris
the village gossip and Mass Zackariah the farmer,
you should have said 'no' to the blue-black man
who asked your hand in hell and marriage.
But we cannot blame him for this residue of balled up tears
lying tumorous on your pancreas;
you loved him and his outside children.

As we roll the stained sheet from under you,
you smile, slide your fingers to the grey hairs down there,
twirl strands like stories tucking you in.
We lift and spread, wipe and powder. In clean, new diapers, you snore off.

Catholic School

There were many days when it rained. There were many days that found me unprotected. There was one particular day, when I was wearing my uniform – white blouse, white

pleated skirt over white full slip, over white cotton brassiere, white cotton panty – and it rained. I walked slowly in the rain – exactly what we were told not to do. *Ladies, walk briskly, move on, move on. Remember rain is an enemy of chastity. Walk briskly ladies.*

But that particular day I walked the way I thought a lady would. She would wear the rain.

I could feel myself moving in this rain – moving in such pure patterns. I lay on the grass and dared it to grow, in such pure patterns. The grass opened like a bed of a thousand scissors and held me up most dangerously from the place I thought this grass would cut again over and over in lady-like slices. I floated outside my clothes, outside whiteness, goodness, crosses, confessions. I prayed for rain and expulsion.

Inheritance

A comedian once said
if you're up between 12 & 3:59,
you're a night person
but if you're up at 4 in the morning
you're a crack addict.

Or you have the curse.
Shut-eye brings visions like confessions.

My mother knew
I was no longer a virgin.
She grew afraid of sleeping,
not wanting to see me
in acrobatic splendour, suspended
by the tip of a tongue, a curious finger.

She knew there was a man
dressed in black
walking down our driveway
way past the hour of visiting.
She woke the neighbours and Christ
when she bawled out,
'Where the hell you think you going?'

My mother's mother watched wrestling
during those ungodly hours,
pounding her fists into the carpet
as if she were ringside and coaching.
After her championship bout she'd vacuum
till the sun came up, singing 'It is well with my soul'
to the hum and sputter of the dust-swallower.

Anything not to sleep.
Anything not to see the lives
of her seven children stretched out
in prophecy. Better not to see.

My mother's youngest sister only sleeps
if the TV is on and loud.
Then she cannot hear the secrets
tumbling under her eyelids.

But my mother insists on sleeping
and always we are hesitant
to board trains and planes.
You can imagine what she's seen.

And me – I sleep and sleep
hoping to inherit the curse
so my poetry may be filled with prophecy.

My Christian Friend

She says she's going to give up sex for Lent,
because after what the Saviour went through,
it's the very least she can do to prove her faith.

So now she's praying for the strength
to keep her legs locked and that's all
she's been praying for.

She thought forty days was too long
so she said God will understand
if she's only strong for a month.

She knows sex before marriage is wrong,
so I ask her what will happen after the month.
After I've been on a diet for a week,
the following week I eat everything I find
that fits into the mouth.

God forbid if she opens her legs
the way I open my mouth.

She says it's the one month sacrifice
that will be written down in the big book,
so if all this works according to her plan
then the sin itself will be cancelled out
by the one month sacrifice.

I tell her isn't it nice that there's flexibility
in Christianity and the Bible is really just
a good book of poetry.

She says she hates when I'm sarcastic
and I'll be really proud of her in the end,
that is, she says, if her oh so sexy man
doesn't wear his red shirt.

Just the thought of him in his red shirt
has her mumbling a prayer while we speak.

Music is Made Out of Smoke

for Lee 'Scratch' Perry

In this cold country
thoughts float freely back

to backs bent under the sun.
The work is never good enough

for a master who seeks blood:
it is said to sweeten the soil.

Am I the slaughtered lamb who poured
kerosene over her body and lit the match

or the burning spear
that began a mystic revolution?

You stand there between my fingers,
sweet reminder of mortality

and in the slanted light between blinds
you diminish into smooth lines

that float like shadows
up to the sky god who reads smoke as sacrifice.

Someone must have had a cigarette in hand,
pulled in

that breath that went searching down corridors of memory
till the whole body

started to heave and convulse.
Blew out

the wail of the ranting reggae man,
suffocating Babylon

on a night like this
when the moon is a black arc too black

for the scattered syncopations
of a back-room melody.

This blue smoke rising in rhythmic curls
crisp and corrugated,

carrying the sound of prophets calling,
the smell of cane fields burning,

is the revolt of memory.

Bought for Half the Original Price

People enter my home and say,
'Oh, but it's so neat,' as if surprised my love
for the imaginary hasn't reduced my living space
into a choir of wailing dirty dishes
and angry laundry,

until the first time visitors spot the shoes
standing in the middle of the room,
filling the empty octagon between green
dining room rug and cheap corner table.
Their eyes stay there long enough for me to know

that even while I'm offering something to drink,
'coffee, tea, maybe?' their response is caught
in the line of impulse between *those shoes*,
maybe she is crazy, am I really that thirsty?
I've thought of putting those shoes away,

but apart from everything else,
I've become attached to their silence:
how they never become spoken; how the eyes
of a visitor possess remarkable restraint even
while a visitor's hand has to include

the spot where those shoes stand into all its
casual gestures; how when the self-indulgent
monologues begin to lose interest, I can disappear.
I can slip my cold feet into those shoes, walk
into a crowded club and be noticed.

I can walk into the night and pretend to own it.
I can kick some balls and wouldn't that be reason
for stimulating conversation: a pot-bellied, too-old-
to-be-picking-up-chicks lecher, scrambling to pick up his seed.
Or I can just walk back to the place I come from.

They'll marvel how I've grown, how foreign has made
my legs strong and toned. Behind my back they'll call me a cow,
say look how she acting *stush* in her glass-bottom boot.
They'll say too much learning has made my head shallow
and that's why they were never interested in books.

I bought those shoes – that are a half size too small –
because of their transparent wedge heel.
Sometimes looking through those shoes I see
my place in this world, growing dark and diminished.
If I put them in the closet then I may forget

there is always the option of leaving, of not listening,
of not opening my door. I may forget how much I love
my legs, how far I've come, how much further left to go.
I may forget the way we look at things through glass,
and see things differently.

IAN STRACHAN

IAN GREGORY STRACHAN has taught English at the University of Massachusetts and is currently Chair of the School of English Studies at the College of the Bahamas. He is the author of the novel *God's Angry Babies* (L. Riener, 1997) and a cultural study, *Paradise and Plantation: Tourism and Culture in the Anglophone Caribbean* (University of Virginia Press, 2002), as well as the plays *Black Crab's Tragedy*, *Diary of Souls* and *No Seeds in Babylon*. Ian Strachan is the founder and director of the Track Road Theatre Company in Nassau.

gods and spirits are summoned through the portal divine

for Gus and Vola

kadak doong doong
kadak doong doong
kadak doong doong
kakkadak doong doong

this is how the drum speaks

kadak doong doong
kadak doong doong
kadak doong doong
kakkadak doong doong

this is how the eyes begin
their easy retreat into the skull
how the muscles tighten and then relax
how the joints prepare themselves
for their starry passengers

kadak doong doong dak dak doong doong
kadak doong doong dak dak doong doong
kadak doong doong dak dak doong doong

this is how the feet repeat the secret steps
how they mark out upon the highways
of the dead and unborn the combination
that unlocks the portal of the gods

doong doong dak dak doong doong
doong doong dak dak doong doong
doong doong dak dak doong doong
kakalak doong doong dak dak doong doong

this is the sound that flings the graves open
that summons the hung, whipped, raped and drowned
to fete on the heads of their living descendants

kadak doong doong dak doong

kadak doong doong dak doong

kadak
                doong doong
                                dak
                                        doong

this is how the gods are remembered
jesus is not one of them

paaa peeee pa-pa-pa-peeeee

spirit children laugh and run in the streets
they race and play, ricocheting rainbows

shango donates lightning
ogun spreads fire
eshu tells tales

paaa peeee pa-pa-pa-peeeee

kadak
                doong doong
                                dak
                                        doong

isn't that the sound of the ship's hold slamming shut?
isn't that the sound of the lights going out?
isn't that the sound of the casket closing?
isn't that the sound of the canons at the slave fort in Guinea?

kadak
                doong doong
                                dak
                                        doong

isn't that the sound of the slaves banging on the hold's door?
isn't that the sound of the slaves banging on the massa's door?
isn't that the sound of the spirits being roused?

kadak
                doong doong
                                dak
                                        doong

of the warriors being called

        kadak

            doong doong

                  dak

                      doong

of the backras takin blows

paaa peeee pa-pa-pa-peeeee

        kadak

            doong doong

                  dak

                      doong

paaa peeee pa-pa-pa-peeeee

the women laugh and show their motion
potcake platoons march past
spirit children ripple rainbows
laughing at eshu's riddles

        kadak

            doong doong

                  dak

                      doong

da-na-na-na-na-naa-na
na naa na-na-na

'DOOOOOOOOOOOOOOOOOOOOOOZZZHHHH!'

da na na naaaa na
na na na na na

dan na na na na naaaaaaaa
dan na naaaaaaa

                  um um-um

                    ... gone, like shadows

Mae Hanna, Grandmother

whip
dawn
of
yesterday

bloodclot'
of misbirth

blood clot
Miss birt'
was
in a
cot
cottage
clutter
wit'
dirt

bloodlight
deat' dawn
grass bed

yes, taday
we ga
cut fiel'
clot peel
cut feel
like deat'
done

whip
dawn
of
yesterday

'daddy
take me
outta
school'

'teacher
wan'
teach her
more dan
da gold
an'
rule'

bloodnight
man gone
mangrove
man grovin'
stronger
erry day

whip
spawn
ship
ho'n
of meagre
pay

whip
dawn
lash
her
nation

whip
gone
gun
on
price
to pay

'pay me
oooooh,
pay me
what you
owe
me'

eyes
alive
heart
dive
body
gone

whip
tongue
strivin

body
whipped
wings
clipped
grave
yard

waitin

whip
dawn
of
yester
day

whip
dawn
of yes,
today

The Dead Their Due

When I get inside
O when I get inside
All my troubles will be over
When I get inside that gate

And you sing the soul to safety
and we mourn the beloved
the suddenly stolen
the child of the long decay
the mother gone to the night

Lay down my dear sister
Lay down and take your rest

Our arms reach heaven from the wailing pews
Our hats are black but grand
Our suits are deep and dark
in the bleached sun,
but they are sharp

I love you
But Jesus love you da best

We are sad, but we are seen

With drums and marching bands,
with the bull frog note of the tuba,
with the sassy laugh of the trumpet,
dance-stepping in time from here to Woodlawn,
Our dresses are white as salt but they are fine
And we travel to that forgetful place
And we suffer
And we celebrate the end
And fall silent,
Struck by Death's disregard
Contemplating the root and terminus
Of our journeys here.

When dear mother used to sing me to sleep

Sing mother to sleep
Sing brother to sleep
Sing sister to sleep
Sing baby to sleep
Sing daddy to sleep

There's a city of light, where there cometh no night,
Tis a city of beauty of untold,
All our treasures are there and its beauty I'll share
When we get to that city of gold

'All Blues': Miles Davis Quintet

for Farah

I

what have the africans made here?
this uncommon sound

colour
dancing in waves
no, droplets
tricklets
undulations
of light

such serenity have they crafted
that even the sky must blush
such figurations of feeling
that even Eshu laughs,
his toes tickled

II

what have the africans made here?
this uncommon sound

how from the bloody field
the stinking pit
the bitter sea
the broken cabin
have they forged
such majesty?

precisely, precisely.

III

what have the africans made here?
this uncommon sound

heart's
deluge
of longing
love
and lullabies
bleak
celestial
elegies,
fireflies ...

IV

praise be to
this groaning,
jubilant thing

sweetest sorrow song
of my soul

ASHE!, I say.

what have the africans made here?
one must wonder at it

they have made us hear
creation's melody.

Haitian Worker, Monday Morning

The sun is a salt thing
It is the only god I know
The sun burns like
Salt in a wound

Salt sun singes skin
Burns and turns my flesh
To water
Salt water I taste in the corners
Of my mouth

It is the only god I know

I kneel before him every day
I bow my head and raise my machete
And let it fall
Bow raise fall
In praise of my god

Who knows the sun better than Isidor?
Roaches, worms
Centipedes, spiders
Crickets, lizards
Run from my god
I am his devotee
I live in his green temple.

Once a day
I raise my head
Only once

I look into the white face
Of my salt god
And it makes me blind.

I see visions
I am washed
Water covers me
And I bow my head again.

Gloriana

here is sorrow enough
for ten tales times ten
and yet this woman,
this silk cotton tree
of a soul
rejoices more in her life
with each salt moon

here is a night so
deep and wide
it swallows song,
but my mother
shuttles an alto
thread of gold
through sackcloth dawns

men raise stiff statues
and scowling monuments
in their own memories,
they order lines composed
so children
never cease to trumpet
each trick and triumph

but what if i said
that this woman,
far from History's
iridescence,
possessing no territories
nor treasure chests
save her soul
has been a sun
lighting worlds?

where are the epics
for our mothers?
when do we print
dollar bills and emboss
them with the faces
of the cerasee sistren
who saved our souls?

here is burden enough
to leave backs brittle
pain enough
to snap the voice's cord
salt enough
to suck the sea fresh ...

and yet, Gloriana stands
guiding the dying
guarding the living
with knees which will not buckle
and a voice that does not break

how many rescues
must you perform?

how many of your sons must
you put in earth?

how many times
must you sow without reaping?

mudda sista fren
how many trips to
the Throne of Grace
must you make
for your children?

these men seeking national
heroes and African kings,
do they have black mothers?
the kind that eat fire
and pass ice for pickney?

let them look to the dark figures
holding the Church up
at the four corners

let them look to the ones
who will wipe the spittle
from their mouths
if Papa Death sneezes ...

this poem says
i have seen what you have borne
in God's name

this poem says
i see what it has all cost
in tears and silent nights
of the owl and the rat

mother of mine
saying prayers
in the four corners
to make hell a home

mother of mine
riding the crest
of syphilitic seas

mother of mine
singing anthems in
aborted dawns and viral rains

mother of mine
knowing too well
the Babylon boots
the hustlers and the whores

BLACK MOTHER OF MINE
LOOK AT ME GROWING IN
THE BEAMS OF YOUR LIFE!

i carry you in me, woman
i see what it has all cost
in tears and silent nights
in sorrow enough
for ten tales times ten
in nights deep and wide
enough to swallow song

i hear you singing
mother of mine
i hear you singing
above the cradle
above the grave

i have seen what it has cost
i have marked this life
of iron you have forged
of rainbows spun
out of sackcloth dawns

I thank creation
for your silk cotton soul

i must share these with you

here, then, is the crux of it

this wave of guava
that embraces me in the backyard
this melody of sugar cane
that makes me shut my eyes
this mellow coolness
of the avocado on my tongue
this terrible delight
of salt water about my shoulders

here is the crux of it

the joy i feel atop this hill
watching sea tickle reef
this giddiness that comes
with the coconut water spilling
this sloppy pleasure i take
in the sugar apple
this fearless gallop
on the crab grass, laughing

here, black woman, is the crux of it:
i must share these with you

JENNIFER RAHIM

JENNIFER RAHIM is a Trinidadian. A writer of poetry, short fiction and criticism, she holds a PhD in English from the University of the West Indies in Jamaica where she is professor of English. Her first collection of poems, *Mothers Are Not The Only Linguists* (New Voices Press, Trinidad, 1992), gained her the Writers Union of Trinidad and Tobago Writer of the Year Award for that year. Her second collection, *Between the Fence and the Forest*, was published by Peepal Tree in 1999. In 2006 she published her first collection of fiction, *Songster and Other Stories* (Peepal Tree). Her poems have appeared in several Caribbean and international journals, including *The Caribbean Writer*, *The Trinidad and Tobago Review*, *The Graham House Review*, *Mangrove*, *The Malahat Review*, *Crab Orchard Review* and *Atlanta Review*, as well as in the anthologies *Crossing Water: Contemporary Poetry of the English-Speaking Caribbean* (Greenfield Review Press, 1992), *Creation Fire: A CAFRA Anthology of Caribbean Women's Poetry* (Sister Vision, 1990) and *Sisters of Caliban: Contemporary Women Poets of the Caribbean* (Azul Editions, 1996).

The Felling of a Tree

When the air is a sharpened blade,
cutting nostrils clean like cutlass steel,
the bush planters pass sleeping houses
(sometimes alone, sometimes in pairs).
They lumber up the mountain road,
their tall tops pound the asphalt smooth.

Sometimes I awake and follow them,
knowing that they go beyond the road's end
into the depths of bearded trees,
where tallness is not neighbours' fences
and bigness is not the swollen houses
that swallow us all.

I follow slowly – my – thinking measured;
my steps behind their thumping boots, steady,
knowing that if I stay in their neat clearings
I will never see, and I want to see the trees,
I want to hear their long silences speaking,
their leaves whispering close to my hungry ears.

I follow, drinking the air like water,
my steps a soft conversation with blades that
cut paths for themselves through the asphalt.
I follow, the strength in my thighs a newness
that makes my feet sprout roots and I think:
this is what tall means.

But when my lips begin to savour my salt,
he looks back, and seeing me growing branches
draws out his cutting steel and sweeps, striking
at my feet, since girls can never become trees.
Turning, I run back down the mountain weeping
like leaves after lashings from rain-forest showers.

Song

to the iron-board's unconsidered flatness, praise
the necessity of clean, well-pressed cotton,
linen, denim, rayon – all fabrics, praise
the vexed countenance of a wrinkled white blouse,

blessed the conscience unable to reject,
in the heat of Monday morning lateness, the homily
preached in any language of a mother's strict
faith in the dogma of a properly ironed blouse,

praise the perfection of well-aligned pleats, razor-
sharp seams, wafer-neat collars and gabardine without a sheen,
praise the uncountable hours over boards that bear
the sizzling cuss-outs of steaming irons,

praise the only crossed legs allowed in her house
that stood the years' heavy-handed mission to
stamp stubborn creases out, praise
the spondaic call to level the terrain of a washed blouse,

all praise the iron-board's appearance each Saturday evening
in the kitchen, chapel of my childhood
where I learnt to meditate the rosary of rhythm, scanning
the lines of her gliding, pressing, thumping hand

that sometimes softly sang, praise
the ever-rising incense of starch and steam,
praise the iron-board's wounded face and its sense
to share memories like a page, without shame,

praise the use-discoloured cover of slow
fading flowers – all praise the unremembered garden
of labour and to the white cotton blouse that now holds me
to the discipline of defying creases, shaping order,

praise the eternal surface that summons a mother,
praise her homely art whose first concern is form,
praise her days spent over convent blouses for a daughter
who never mastered her hand's command of an iron

praise be the iron-board, tapered at end
as if to ride the unruly surf, or
to make the markings of a pen

Lady Lazarus in the Sun

I

It must always be done
this business of rising from the grave
like some stubborn sun

I practise on instruction
Just do it
put my shoes on, take up
the weight a body gathers
and walk across dark waters

No real miracle
even with irons for sandals
walk the Atlantic light

But I have to manage it –
with my skin
watered down to brightness
as a salvation

My feet are a history
heavy with El Dorado gold,
brown sugar madness
ole' time sailor sweetness

Watch how I step into the ring
showing my motion
my body a beauty,
a prize,
prised too early
for a taste of sugar
dumplin,
sugar
cake
down the middle
passage
way
from darkness

Smile please lady
forget the bitter taste of cane

II

at least once a month
this coming back from the slips –
bleeding the agony of blank
the broken plank
the free fall –
O lord my brain, my brain
howls an unspeakable knowledge
of unremembered things
I try to learn its language

This blackout, a saviour –
dark mother when you poke
prod, probe me –
the blank you read in me
the giddy decline to nothing
the going under I feel
is your judgment text

Read between the blank
for stealing my sex

III

Another month and
I have come back again
and you are pleased thinking
soon she will be breakfast-toast-
brown again
ready for jam again,
milk in your coffee again
currency
playing the fool on TV
selling island sun
Vat 19 rum
with natural coppertone
mildly processed curls-

preferred girl
And I will be, as you want me,
grateful for my fix
callaloo theory,
carnival baby, global
everybody
just easy

IV

But listen
I have lived with the dead
seven times seventy years
rotten anxiety shrouds me
bones rattle in my body
a girl sucking her thumb
still moans in me

Here
put your fingers where they
have pierced –
it *is* really me
don't be afraid
now you've had your piece

I come into the light
my skin paled in this grave
of dark usage

No, I will not be dancing
this time
to tunes that play me
for dead
skin fried crisp as KFC
or shaking my sugar bumsey
because I have done it again
heard the call,
seen the light and said

Alleluia

said

Yes

picked up my bed, Amen
and kept on walking

V

I do this rising business
like I wash my body
sun my history
air my wounds in the wind
take off my death again
my dress again
stand the fierce heat of visibility
without sun-block
without mushroom umbrella
without Ray-Ban
stare straight the face
of golden brightness
becoming my Kali self
slowly
learning to stand
on the chest of my enemy –
take back my sun again
becoming the dark past brown again
the woman no longer under

I will love my darkness well

Miss I-Tired

I hear her calling to the houses she knows.
At Lydia's gate, always stopping for a chat
and rest before she takes up her weight again,
holding the same pain at her waist, her head
leading her feet onward to the next station.
Dotsy's name sings out. A brief exchange.
She teases Nathaniel, coaxes him to speak.
He plays her game and pronounces a string
of undecipherable words and her joy erupts,
embracing the entire mountain. Complete.
She moves on. Behind her, the entire ocean
straddles her back – all the time going up
to a home way past my seeing. Her eternal
prayer showering Rose Hill – *Lord, I so tired!*

For the Seeds that Wither

This is a beg pardon
for the seeds that wither
and get choked out before they flower

those fragile ones eager to bear
that rock-heart and shallow-mind
kill dead long before their time

For the unborn and all things just
beginning that meet sudden dry season
today I beg pardon

For all seeds that start to grow
in the look-at-my-crosses spots of bird-drop
like concrete crack and old chamber pot

For the paw-paw plant that claim a space
right in Miss Mary rose-garden
and get root out for being too brazen

this is a chant to break the back
of the jumbie who busy building fences
to keep *them* in and *us* always out

like Amado Diallo who eat police bullet
for holding up a wallet in a pasture
he dreamt might to be greener

For all those we slam the life door on
who pass by without being mourned
today I beg pardon

This is a prayer for the down and out
the coke-heads and gone-crazy
the ones whose courage-tank run empty

This is a hymn for women like Bajan Patsy
that life and men beat up on
till body and soul-case split like a pod

This is a prayer that at least someone
will mourn and temples of rebirth rise
where their limbs meet with earth

Today I beg pardon
for seeds that wither and die
before they get a chance at life

The Wild Cat

July 22nd

The wild cat was prowling again last night.
I heard her padded paws pacing the veranda.
I didn't leave the light on. That must have attracted her –
she likes playing in the dark. It is her time
to put on her amber torches to search me out.
The truth is we have been looking for each other,
only I am reluctant to let her in the house.
I think of the ruction and scandal she will cause.
Mostly, I fear she will devour me;
but she is growing impatient. Some mornings
I see her prints on my door and once
she left a dead thing on the chair
where I sit to watch the ocean lap the shore.
But change is in the air. To my surprise,
I left my key in the lock last night.

The Mango

I am told the great Buddha found rest
in the shade of a mango tree,

that the fruit is food of the gods
and the blossoms Cupid's love arrows

or Manmatha's darts. Or else the mango
is the wish-granting tree, and its juice

cleanses the body of impurities.
For Goodison its sweetness is poetry.

I wish I'd known these stories
when I was a girl among its branches

begging freedom from an ugly love,
eating so I might never touch the ground.

Perhaps this knowing is right on time
like Saraswati's gift of learning,

for now I know my hard passage
to be blessed since my child's prayer

rose in the fragrance of heaven,
and today poems flow in my blood

becoming sunlight with each season
as the ambrosial flesh of mangoes.

A Grandfather Sings

A bajhan breaks the dawn.
Grandfather paces a yard swept bald
with care, singing India
into his granddaughter's ear.

His voice strains past
walls where time gnaws on long
as a carili vine strung with bitter bulbs
for cleansing bad blood.

He sings the only lullaby he knows –
a prayer from his childhood mornings,
his mother veiled at the jhandis
pleading to gods he no longer serves.

He places their language on her tongue
while eyes open wide in cocoa houses
that reek the scent of his labour.
He reads understanding in her babble,

hugs her close, breathing gratitude
for newness strange as the communion
in her veins makes her another race.
One day she will speak her own words.

So he gives her the India he remembers
and wonders at the other tightening
in her curls as light rains through leaves,
blessing them with many, many arms.

My mother took it

Grenada, August 2003

My mother took it. Aaron standing with me
before Annadale Falls. A miracle shot really:
an August evening after rain, the light fading,
and mummy awkward with the camera shifting
this way and that, and we restrained by smiles
forgot to say *flash!* She wouldn't take another.
For all my pleading simply said, *It'll be fine.*
With that being that, we climbed single file
like pilgrims leaving a shrine. Now, there it is,
with me wherever I go, the way we carry love:
Aaron leaning gently on my side, behind us
a pierced dark gushing water anoints his head,
and both of us beaming out at the woman
fumbling with the camera whose light was on.

Saint Francis and the Douen

after reading Galway Kinnell

The head
sheltered by a great mushroom hat
holds the secret of all things beginning
and the wisdom of their endings.
Hidden there
is the knowledge of mysteries unbaptised,
tiny, faceless creatures –
those knots of possibility are the dread
beneath the hat.
Hidden there
is a mouth that cries in the forests,
calling the living to step
beyond the boundary of their seeing;

but sometimes it is necessary
to reach out and cradle the child,
and tell again in touch and sweet lullaby
of its loveliness and wonderful promise;
as Saint Francis did
when he followed the small voice
that beckoned him from the darkness,
then stooped low to where the infant sat
naked on a wet riverbank,
swaddled in the mud of all things beginning;
and reaching to take the child into his arms
he saw his face look back at him,
right there, from water's surface,
and in that moment's recognition
found again the gift of self-blessing –
for all things rise to life again, from within,
in the waters of self-blessing;

so the Saint gently removed the hat
in a sunbathed spot witnessed by the river,
the earth, the trees and the passing breeze,
and with healing touch and soft song
sang of the infant's perfect loveliness;
from the tender head and troubled brow,

the shy, half-formed face
and the small wounded heart,
he blessed the whole length of the body;
from the up-stretched arms
to the strange, backward turn of the feet,
he blessed their high intelligence
to brave the abandoned places
only to save what is theirs alone to give,
blessed again and again that perfect beauty
until the child became sunlight,
forever shining within –
of self-blessing.

Index of First Lines

Index of Titles